What to Do
Until the Lawyer Comes

STEPHAN LANDSMAN is an assistant professor of law at Cleveland-Marshall College of Law in Cleveland, Ohio. Formerly he was an attorney with the Monroe County Legal Assistance Corporation in Rochester, New York. He has also been a part-time instructor in political science at the State University of New York at Brockport. Professor Landsman and his wife are both practicing attorneys.

DONALD MCWHERTER is a professor of political science at the State University of New York at Brockport. His areas of specialization are American politics and public law. In 1976, Professor McWherter was awarded the state university chancellor's award for excellence in teaching.

ALAN PFEFFER is an assistant professor of political science at the State University of New York at Brockport, specializing in political theory. Mr. Pfeffer received the state university chancellor's award for excellence in teaching in 1974.

Contents

Preface

Before the last century, the study of law was considered a basic part of a person's education. Blackstone's famous commentaries on the laws were best sellers in colonial America, and there were innumerable analyses and updatings of his work. Quotations from Roman law were liberally sprinkled in any discussion of public affairs; indeed, acquaintance with Roman legal institutions was an indispensable element of any gentleman's intellectual training. As the French observer Alexis de Tocqueville noted, in the United States everything became a law case and everyone was a lawyer.

In our century, law has been removed from basic education. Not that people are any less interested in legal problems: Be it marijuana or school integration by busing, crime in the streets or in the White House, legal issues continue to dominate our political and intellectual lives. Growing enrollment in law schools indicates the unceasing fascination the law holds for Americans. Nor is this fascination unjustified. Not only is law central to our lives, but its influence and impact are constantly expanding. Courts are deciding more cases—and more kinds of cases—than ever before. The number and nature of possible public and private legal relationships have increased exponentially.

Yet, this involvement with legal matters no longer evidences itself in a direct concern with the study of law. Our rich tradition of relying on law and the judicial processes not only to regulate certain forms of activity but also to restrict governmental invasion of our private lives has not translated itself into a substantial effort by citizens to understand what law is really all about. Instead, it is too often dismissed as a dry, technical subject best left to attorneys.

Our purpose in writing this book is to return law to the people, with whom it belongs. We do not seek to displace the numerous scholarly textbooks or academic studies of law that have been produced over the years. Rather, we wish to present a straightforward treatment of law as an aspect of daily life and normal society, law as it relates to the ordinary citizen, law as an institution as commonplace and unremarkable as the family or the economy. No one reading this book will receive any training as a lawyer. We hope that our readers will receive a broader outlook on a significant part of their lives.

To help meet this end, and avoid the dry abstraction so associated with law, we have chosen examples and cases with which most people are familiar: buying a car, renting an apartment, and so on. This should *not* be interpreted as an indication that the book is designed as a "Do-It-Yourself" guide to the practice of law. No single book could possibly accomplish that (students spend three years in law school before they are eligible to practice law, and the Chief Justice of the United States says that many of them are still incompetent). Instead, we hope to inspire further interest in law and provide a basis from which to critically examine our legal system.

Law has been called the greatest creation of civilized humanity. Certainly it is an essential part of our society and of our lives, and we would all do well to understand this part of our culture. This book is designed to serve that purpose.

In the course of writing this book, we have incurred many debts we are happy to acknowledge. We are particularly grateful to our friend, critic, and typist Adele Catlin, without whose aid this book would never have been completed. Professors L. S. Tao and Philip Katz of the State University of New York at Brockport, and Professor Leo Pfeffer of Long Island University were kind enough to read part or all of our manuscript and to make several valuable suggestions. Eddy Hoey, a political science student at Brockport College, was most helpful in proofreading the preliminary draft and final chapters. Finally, we would like to thank Mary Ellen Travis, former editor at Anchor Press, who encouraged us to begin this book, and Elizabeth Knappman, our editor, who encouraged us to finish it. Naturally, we assume full responsibility for any errors of omission or commission that appear in the book.

What to Do
Until the Lawyer Comes

1

The Nature of Law

Law is one of the most powerful and respected concepts of our civilization. A "law-abiding citizen" is an admirable individual; an "outlaw" is the villain in a Western, whose defeat in the end is assured and deserved. Of course, since the Revolution, Americans have agreed that there are times when the law must be disobeyed in the name of a higher truth, but such occasions are rare. The reaction to the Vietnam War resisters, many of whom violated the law for the sake of conscience, shows how cautious most Americans are in accepting this kind of action.

When it comes to specifics, however, we find that there are exceptions to our respect for the law. Jaywalking is illegal in most places, but few people would want to see jaywalkers in jail. Many drivers go a few miles an hour faster than the legal speed limit without feeling particularly guilty about it; if asked, they would probably say that they support law and order, but that no one takes these little violations seriously.

This response is not simply hypocrisy. In fact, it raises a question that has troubled lawyers, legal philosophers, and sociologists for centuries: what is the law? Are laws that are still on the books but that everyone ignores really laws? In some states, for instance, old prohibitions against witchcraft remain unrepealed, but no judge or jury today would ever convict anyone of breaking those regulations. On the other hand, the police sometimes enforce rules that are not officially "laws." In Beverly Hills, for example, the home of many movie and television stars, patrol cars protect the privacy of their famous residents by picking up for "vagrancy" anyone on foot in the area. These people are driven to the police station, away from the residential section, and then released. Is it accurate, then, to say that it is against the law to stroll in Beverly Hills? Or is this policy something other than law?

There are other kinds of problems in defining the law. In 1963, in a case called *Gideon* v. *Wainright*, the Supreme Court of the United States declared that anyone on trial for a serious offense had the right to a lawyer, and if he could not afford one, the court should provide one at the government's expense. This ruling meant that it would be a violation of the law to convict someone who did not have a lawyer. But what about people who had been tried and convicted without lawyers before 1963? Were they being held in prison against the law? The Court said that they were, and ordered that they be given new trials or released. But did that mean that the people who had conducted the original trials, the judges who allowed the trials to proceed without providing an attorney for the defendant, were *themselves* guilty of crimes? Were the prison officials guilty of kidnaping? Not at all. It is true that the trials were improperly run and therefore their verdicts were invalid, but nobody could have known that until the Supreme Court said so. The written law had not been changed (the decision was based on an interpretation of the Fourteenth Amendment to the Constitution, which was almost a century old), but it now had a new meaning.

If a law can change without being rewritten, though, how can anybody know if he or she is obeying the law or not? This is not just a philosopher's question. Many lawsuits come to court over issues like that. Two people sign a contract and then argue over exactly what it means. Both agree they should follow the contract. Their problem is deciding what the contract actually says so that they *can* follow it. To interpret the contract, they go to court, where the judge decides what the law is. Only at that point, if one of them refuses to obey the court, is he breaking the law.

What, then, is the law? In general, people have taken three different approaches to answering this question. The first group takes the common-sense attitude. To find out what the law is, ask the ones who make it. This group defines the law in terms of its sources. Once we have identified the lawmakers, we can easily determine the content of the law.

Scholars trained in the social sciences adopt a second method. Identifying the people who make the laws, they say, is to go about the whole thing backward. How can we decide who the lawmakers are if we do not first know what the law is? No, the only way to understand the law is to investigate what it is that the law accomplishes in society. Once we know what the law does, we can distinguish what is law from what is not. Then, and only then, can we go about describing and analyzing the entire legal system.

Philosophers look at the question still another way. The most important fact about the law, they say, is not that certain people make it or that it performs certain functions, but that people obey it. If we, as citizens, interest ourselves in the law, it is because we are concerned with our position with regard to it. The correct place to begin our study, therefore, is with the reasons people have (or ought to have) for following the law.

The Sources of Law

If the average citizen were asked, "Who makes the law?" he would probably answer, "The government." This common-sense approach to the question has not escaped legal scholars. "Legal positivism" or "analytic jurisprudence," a theory associated especially with John Austin (1790–1859), insists that law is nothing more or less than the orders the sovereign group in a society gives to the rest of the population. When the government commands, the people obey.

To say that law is the command of the sovereign does not mean that we must go to Congress every time there is a dispute over the law. The government sets up such agencies as the police to enforce the law and judges to interpret it. Ultimately, though, laws are written by and can be changed by the legislature alone. Only the legislature is a source of true law. When people, or even the police, adhere to some principle that did not originate with the legislative body, then, whatever else it is they may be doing, they are not following the law. According to the positivist theory, to find out what the law is in any specific case, we simply look it up in the statute books, where it should be clearly written down for us to read and obey.

Legal positivists, to be sure, recognize the fact that not all laws are clearly drafted. In such cases, they agree, a policeman or judge will have leeway in interpreting the official law. Moreover, there are many customary legal principles, called "common law" in the Anglo-American system, that were not actually legislated but are followed anyway. Supporters of the positivist theory maintain that these exceptions, although they exist, do not disprove their theory, since the legislatures, by permitting these conditions to continue, have in effect endorsed these interpretations and traditions, and thus made them into law.

Legal positivism is an attractive theory. It is simple, clear-cut, and fits in with our common-sense view of the matter. Naturally laws are the regulations enacted by the government; indeed, at first glance it is hard to see why anyone might disagree with this approach.

Most lawyers do, in practice, adhere to some type of

positivist theory. In law schools it is adopted almost as a matter of course as law students are trained to search out relevant statutes and court decisions to answer legal questions. Many legal philosophers also accept positivist theory or some variant thereof. Yet there are difficulties with positivism, some of which are technical, others not. For instance, if law is the command of the sovereign, how do we explain contracts? Contracts, as we shall see in Chapter 5, are agreements people make voluntarily, creating their own obligations. The law does order us to fulfill our contracts, but it is we, not the government, who decide their terms. This reality does not easily fit into standard positivist theory.

Another objection to positivism can be based on moral grounds. Positivist theory does not distinguish between good and bad laws, between laws that should be obeyed and those, like the racial laws of Nazi Germany, that are abhorrent to basic decency. For many people, especially believers in natural law, which we shall discuss shortly, this ethical neutrality is unacceptable. Further, there is the problem, already mentioned, of the laws that are on the books but not actually enforced. Are these really laws, as positivists maintain? It seems rather artificial to classify them together with regulations that are observed in practice.

Indeed, some investigators reject the entire positivist approach as too artificial. The real question, they argue, is not what some lawbook moldering in the state archives may say, but what the police and the courts do about it. Law is whatever is enforced.

Following this idea, scholars belonging to a school of social science named "behavioralism" have begun examining, on a statistical basis, just how laws operate in the daily world. They have discovered, for instance, that a person who can get out on bail is less likely to be convicted of a crime than a poorer one, charged with the same crime, who cannot; or that juries in urban areas are likely to award higher verdicts in accident cases than those in rural districts. Similarly, a study of the Washington, D.C., court system showed that certain judges gave harsher sentences than others on crimes of violence but were more lenient with "white collar crimes" (such as embezzlement). These realities, say the behavioralists, not the official codes, are the true law.

This notion draws support from some distinguished practitioners of the law, such as Justice Oliver Wendell Holmes (1841–1935), who said:

> When we study law we are not studying a mystery but a well-known profession. We are studying what we shall want in order to appear before judges, or to advise people in such a way as to keep them out of court. . . . The object of our study, then, is prediction, the prediction of the incidence of the public force through the instrumentality of the courts. . . . The prophecies of what the courts will do in fact, and nothing more pretentious, are what I mean by the law.

Legal behavioralists often connect their approach to the development of modern science. Like science, law uses the results of past cases in order to predict the future. A law case, in a sense, is an experiment: the parties are testing to find out what will happen in certain conditions that are similar to past ones but may differ in a significant variable. Thus, one of the major thrusts of behavioral research has been to predict the votes of Supreme Court justices by analyzing statistically their judicial ideologies. This technique can, at least in theory, be applied to any legal encounter.

Like legal positivism, behavioralism has a strong common-sense appeal. We are more interested in what courts actually do than in what they are supposed to do according to written regulations. Therefore it seems reasonable to focus our attention on this behavior rather than on legislative statutes. Legal positivism may well be technically correct, but behavioralism appears to be more relevant to the average citizen.

Another school of thought, however, who call themselves legal "realists," assert that even the behavioralists are too artificial and removed from actuality. When a person goes to a lawyer, he is not interested in statistical generalities but in persuading a specific judge and a specific jury to come to a favorable decision. The individual is not a scientist, seeking predictive probabilities or demonstrable hypotheses. He is an individual with a problem, and all he wants is to get the problem resolved as quickly and as efficiently as possible. For him, the law is no more and no less than the resolution of his difficulties.

Consequently, legal realists turn their attention from mathematical averages to particular cases. They look at the psychological makeup of a judge, the prejudices of a juror, the personal experiences of a policeman. Why does a judge sentence one criminal to several years in prison and, the next day, suspend the sentence of another person convicted of exactly the same crime? The reason may be no more profound than that on the second day the judge's child was admitted to an outstanding law school. A juror may vote against a plumber in a civil suit simply because he was once charged seventy-five dollars to repair a leaky faucet. Clearly, neither lawbooks nor statistical charts can enable one to deal with these kinds of situations. Law, for the realists, is as much a knowledge of people as it is of statutes.

Undoubtedly, considerations of the successes of the judge's children or a juror's sink seem out of place in studying the majesty of the law, but the realists say an honest investigator cannot ignore them. They dismiss the image of the lofty, impartial judge as part of the "cult of the robe," the blind semiworship of the law that exists in our society. Of course, most judges try to be fair, and this effort is an important element of their psychological outlook. It is, though, only one element, not the whole picture.

At this point, many specialists in law protest vigorously.

No one denies that a policeman is more likely to give out tickets if he had a fight with his wife that morning, but it does seem to be going too far to include his marital relations in the study of law. The trouble with all these approaches is that their practitioners are so caught up in examining the details of the administration of the law that they have forgotten the essence of law. It is to this essence we must return.

Believers in "natural law" insist that law cannot be understood unless one takes into account its moral basis. True law is the application of general ethical principles to specific cases. It is the weighing and evaluation of the facts in the context of basic concepts of fairness and justice. Unless these ideas are grasped, law will appear to be merely an arbitrary collection of assorted rules, not the system of conduct that it really is.

At first glance, the natural lawyers admit, their approach might seem too idealistic, but to reject their view is, they believe, little more than superficial cynicism. Only a cynic (or a dogmatic positivist) could really believe that judges pay no attention to justice in their deliberations. The same is true of juries. In eighteenth-century Britain, for example, the penalty for picking pockets was death. As a result, jurors simply refused to convict anyone of that crime, no matter how clear the evidence, because they thought the punishment was too severe. Abolitionist jurors in New England in the era before the Civil War were equally reluctant to enforce the fugitive-slave laws. The law said that a master could recover any runaway slave he could prove belonged to him. As far as the juries in the free states were concerned, though, no proof was ever sufficient. Clearly, these men were following natural law and morality rather than written law.

Advocates of the theory of natural law recognize that many existing laws are immoral. Their position is that these enactments are not truly "law" at all, but acts of oppression enforced by violence alone; in the long run, these measures are either overthrown or disregarded.

An important aspect of natural-law theory is its practical implications. If a "law" that violates natural law is not really a law, then people are not morally obliged to obey it. Natural law, in other words, provides a justification for resistance and revolution. Indeed, it may well be our duty to combat immoral acts of the government, especially if it requires us to co-operate. From the American Revolution to the Vietnam War, opponents of official policies have appealed to natural law to justify their rebellion.

The positivists and their offshoots, behavioralists and realists, are not persuaded by these arguments. They admit that some laws are immoral, but they do not consider that fact relevant to the study of law. Moral individuals and responsible citizens may well find it necessary to disobey the law; the job of lawyers, however, is to study the law, not to evaluate it by their personal standards, and the two activities must be kept distinct. Believers in natural law, on the other hand, maintain that separating law from justice empties the law of its true meaning.

The Functions of Law

The apparently interminable dispute between natural lawyers and positivists (with their behavioralist and realist allies) has led other legal scholars to seek out new approaches to their subject. For people trained in the social sciences especially, it has seemed preferable to study what role law plays in a society before trying to define it more exactly. After all, we can all agree more or less on what the law is, even if there are definitional problems in borderline cases. The real question is, what does the law do?

According to adherents of "historical jurisprudence," the question is easily answered. Any specific law is an enactment, written in the past, designed to guide a person's present and future behavior. Law in general is the legacy of our ancestors, their advice on how to conduct our lives and our social order. It is the total of the past experience of a nation, the lessons of its history, the heritage of its wisdom. It is the element of stability in a rapidly changing world.

Consider the provision, in the First Amendment to the Constitution, guaranteeing freedom of the press. When it was adopted, in 1791, its authors could have had no conception of modern newspapers, of television and radio, much less of "Deep Throat" or of the Pentagon Papers. But they were working within a tradition. Over generations, people had learned that governments often try to suppress ideas and news unfavorable to them and their policies. Over generations, citizens had fought and struggled to win for themselves the right to say and print what they believed. The First Amendment summarized their experience, enshrined it in the law, and passed it on to their descendants. For the supporters of historical jurisprudence, this case typifies the nature of law.

This theory of the law was summarized most eloquently by the British statesman Edmund Burke (1729–97): ". . . the idea of inheritance furnishes a sure principle of conservation and a sure principle of improvement. . . . We receive, we hold, we transmit our government and our privileges. . . ."

Burke refers to improvement, but it does seem at first glance that this conception of law leaves no room for change. If the law embodies the past, then one can no more change the law than one can change the past. Most historical theorists, however, do not go that far. They admit that changing conditions may require changes in the law, but they maintain that if the changes are to be effective, they must reflect our experience with a problem, not our forecasting of one. Like the realists, though for very different reasons, the historical school distrusts abstract principles of law. Law, it insists, must reflect life.

Thus, believers in historical jurisprudence tend to be conservative in their political views. ("Law and order" is a slogan most often used by conservatives.) Law, they say, the great preserver of our social heritage, provides order in a world in flux. There are lawyers, no doubt, who reject this notion and insist that law can be used as an instrument of social change, not merely to defend the status quo. Still, most lawyers probably are, and have been, conservatives. To this extent at least, the principles of historical jurisprudence are in keeping with reality.

Lawyers of a reformist bent are often more sympathetic to the "sociological theory of law," for it focuses on law as an adaptive mechanism and not simply as a preservative one. Unlike the historians, sociologists are interested in the ways law changes to fit new conditions. Law, according to this theory, is not the sum of a society's experience; rather, it is the way society copes with new problems.

We can see the basis for the sociological theory most clearly if we look at how laws are made in Congress and other legislative bodies. When a new situation develops among some citizens, they begin demanding action from their representatives. The legislature proceeds to investigate the matter, and then proposes new laws to deal with the problems. If there are no new problems, then there are no calls for action, and so few laws are passed. In practice, of course, there are always enough problems around to keep Congress busy.

Sociologists argue that the same process can also be seen at work in the court system. For instance, under a legal concept called "standing to sue," no one can bring a case to court unless he can show that he is personally harmed to a noticeable extent by the action claimed to be illegal. Standing was therefore normally restricted to individuals with a substantial financial interest in an affair. However, the twentieth century has seen the rise of such organized interest groups as the National Association for the Advancement of Colored People (NAACP) and the Ameri-

can Civil Liberties Union (ACLU), which want judicial
action on their broad social goals and not merely on individual complaints. The courts have responded by enlarging
the concept of standing to enable a group to represent the
interests of other concerned individuals even if no single
person can demonstrate substantial personal damage. For
the sociological theorist, this example is typical of the
over-all development of the law.

Most important of all for the sociologists is the work of
the administrative agencies (see Chapter 8). These "quasi-
judicial bodies," as they are called, such as the Federal
Communications Commission and the Securities and Exchange Commission, were established with the express
purpose of adapting the law to fit specific conditions.
Congress set out over-all guidelines, and then gave the
agencies the power to make and enforce more specific
rules. If one does not like the decision of a commission, it
is true, he can go to court. But the courts have usually
held that, so long as a commission follows a reasonable
procedure and is fair, its decision must be upheld (even if
the judge himself does not like it). The reason for giving
so much power to these commissions is to enable them to
respond to new problems as they develop, without having
to go to Congress or to court every time something un-
foreseen comes up. In other words, flexibility is their key
feature.

According to the sociologists, the historians have the
whole thing backward. Nobody needs the law to solve
problems of the past. These have already been answered,
and people can know the rules in such situations without
having to go to court for help. It is when the case is
different, when there are no "precedents" (the legal term
used to refer to previous relevant court decisions), that we
appeal to the law for guidance. Law helps us accommodate ourselves to innovations.

The historical theorists respond by asking where judges,
agencies, or legislators get their ideas for dealing with

these new situations. If they simply invent them to suit their own preferences, then there would be little point in hiring a lawyer to argue the case; we would just present the problem to the proper authority and wait for a reply. In reality, of course, this is not how even administrative agencies operate. They listen to lawyers argue over the intent of the legislature, over past procedures, over the meaning of the law, and then make a judgment. Thus, they are appealing to the past for guidance.

While the historians and the sociologists debate this matter, they are both denounced as tools of the system by still a third group of social analysts, the "radicals." The radical theory of law insists that conventional legal philosophies actually distract attention from the reality of law. For the radicals, the basic truth these theorists cover up is that law is a tool of the ruling class to preserve its dominance in society.

> The executive of the modern State is but a committee for managing the common affairs of the whole bourgeoisie. . . . Your very ideas are but the outgrowth of the conditions of your bourgeois property, just as your jurisprudence is but the will of your class made into a law for all, a will, whose essential character and direction are determined by the economic conditions of existence of your class.

These words are from the *Communist Manifesto*, of Karl Marx (1818–83) and Friedrich Engels (1820–95). However, it is not only Marxists and Communists, but most other radicals as well, who agree on the major thrust of this theory. If we look at the structure and operations of government, they say, we easily see that it is big business that finances election campaigns, big business that can afford lobbies in Congress and high-powered lawyers in court, and big business that provides jobs to defeated legislators or retired government officials. Naturally, the government and its laws serve the interests of their supporters.

The radicals also point to psychological and social factors. Judges, congressmen, and other major bureaucrats are rarely chosen from among the workers, minority groups, or even small businessmen. By and large, the government is staffed with upper-middle-class and upper-class types, such as corporate executives, Wall Street lawyers, or the heirs of wealthy families. These people may be honest and sincere (although some of them are not), but they still cannot escape their own backgrounds. They have never been unemployed, or in debt, and they simply do not understand the point of view of most Americans. Instead, they write and interpret the laws in terms of their own experiences, emphasizing the importance of security for property and ignoring human needs and problems that simply have never arisen in their own lives.

Moreover, the whole purpose of law is to preserve order and justice as it is defined in our society. Securing order and justice, though, means strengthening the current system, which, of course, favors the interests of the wealthy and the privileged. So even reforms designed to improve the conditions of the poor and weak actually help the rich by calming discontent and preventing revolution. For a radical, any change in the law short of revolution is a fraudulent effort—conscious or unconscious—to buy off the oppressed rather than free them.

Historical and sociological theorists, as we would expect, reject the radical argument almost entirely. Nevertheless, this should not obscure the similarity in approaches the three theories utilize. All are *functional* theories; that is, they focus attention on the way law works to keep the society operating satisfactorily (at least, a radical would say, satisfactorily for the ruling class). All three lead their supporters to study the interaction of law with other social institutions—government, economy, family—rather than law in isolation. For this reason, they are more attractive to social scientists than the first group of definitional theories, whereas practicing lawyers usually prefer the positivist or realist approaches, which lead directly into the study of legislative and courtroom experiences, where the attorney feels at home.

Legitimacy of the Law

For some investigators of the legal system, neither lawyers nor social scientists are asking the right questions. Law is important, they point out, because it is followed; no one is really interested in "dead-letter" laws that are on the books but ignored. Furthermore, we must distinguish between law and pure force, between the policeman and the robber. When a robber commands us to turn over our money, we obey him, but we do not consider this a legal transaction. Law has a quality philosophers refer to as "legitimacy"; that is, we think that we *ought* to obey it. As to why do we think this, philosophers differ.

Some argue that the legitimacy of law is based on consent. People obey the law because they agreed to do so in exchange for the benefits of society. According to this theory, law is a kind of contract, and adherents of this view are called "social-contract theorists." Life without society, they point out, would be unbearable; everyone would be stealing from everyone else and no one would be safe. Consequently, people come to recognize that they need laws to regulate their behavior, and a government to enforce those laws. They therefore agree among themselves to establish a certain form of authority, and to obey it as long as it continues to do its job. This is, of course, the theory expressed in the Declaration of Independence.

In reality, few people other than naturalized citizens ever actually promise to obey the law in any formal way. The social-contract theorists argue, though, that most of us act as if we had made such a promise and have thus in effect given our consent. Most Americans seem to accept the idea that while it is all right to disagree with a law, we should obey it if it has been legally passed by our government. Even those who feel they cannot obey the law because of their consciences usually are prepared to accept the penalties the law imposes. Surely, maintain these theorists, this attitude demonstrates that persons feel obligated by their own agreement to follow the law, or be punished if they do not.

Moreover, in a democracy, there is the additional fact that people participate in the making of laws by voting, working in political campaigns, writing letters to congressmen, and so on. Such activity would not make much sense if it were not tied to a pledge to accept the final outcome even if one disagrees with it. Getting involved is itself a form of consent.

This unwritten contract is a two-way arrangement. Just as the people acknowledge a duty to the government, the government has a duty to its citizens. It must guarantee them law and order, peace and justice. If a regime cannot or will not fulfill its part of the bargain, the contract ceases to be valid, and anarchy or revolution results.

The social-contract theory was very popular in the seventeenth and eighteenth centuries, and underlies not only the Declaration of Independence but also the Constitution and most state constitutions. In time, however, objections raised against it led to the development of alternative explanations of the legitimacy of laws. One criticism is of particular interest here: that the social-contract theory is insufficiently realistic, that it is too formal and abstract.

Many individuals first coming upon the social-contract theory react much as the British skeptical philosopher Hume (1711–76) did two centuries ago: "But would these reasoners look abroad into the world, they would meet with nothing that in the least corresponds to their ideas or can warrant so refined and philosophical a system. . . ." A pretty fantasy, perhaps, but the social-contract notion has no relation at all to anything that ever happened.

Why, then, do we follow the law? Because we were brought up to do so. This "traditionalist theory" attributes our respect for the law to the customs of the society in which we grow up. There is no voluntary consent involved here. As soon as children are old enough to understand, they are taught to be good, to follow the rules, to listen to the policeman, to honor the government and the flag. They learn to regard violation of law as evil per se, regardless of which law was violated or for what reasons. By the time most people are old enough to make their own decisions, they are so accustomed to accepting the laws that it never even occurs to them that anyone might raise the question "why?" They follow the law because it is the "right" thing to do.

As evidence for the truth of their theory, traditionalists suggest that we observe the psychological reactions of an individual who does break the law. He does not act like someone who has merely broken a contract, as the social-contract theorists assume he should. Instead, he behaves guiltily. He may be ashamed and try to conceal the crime, or he may swagger and pretend to be proud of having rejected accepted standards of the society, but in either case there is clearly an irrational, emotional feeling about it which must be the result of childhood training. Surely the social-contract theory cannot explain this response.

Thus, the traditionalists argue that the social-contract theory of law is too mechanical. It assumes that people behave logically, that law develops through reason, that individuals think for themselves about issues. In fact, say the traditionalists, none of these propositions is true. We never really decide to obey the law—we simply do what we were trained to do.

"Public-interest theorists" agree with the traditionalists that social-contract theory is too artificial, but their concern is with its individualistic premises. According to social-contract theory, each individual agrees personally to accept the law. The trouble with this idea, say the democrats, is that it permits us to ignore the wishes and interests of our neighbors and fellow citizens. The theory emphasizes only selfish motives; it leaves out group considerations. More specifically, it neglects the whole question of the good of the people.

The basic purpose of law is to serve the common welfare. The very fact that people organize themselves into a social system instead of living in an anarchic, or lawless, society demonstrates that they are interested in other people besides themselves. In every country, there are laws that are necessary for the interest of the people as a whole and not just of a few individuals. In fact, this idea of the public interest is precisely the difference between general laws, which apply to everyone, and private contracts, which deal with the particular goals of the signatories. A "social contract" is almost a contradiction in terms.

The distinction between the public good and private self-interest is basic to law. Examine, for instance, the law requiring new automobiles to have pollution-control devices. Everyone, no doubt, is in favor of clean air. However, it is not necessarily in the self-interest of each individual to install such a device on his or her car. A person might reason this way: "Pollution-control apparatus will cost me extra money, so I will not buy one unless it is in my personal interest. I agree that it is in my best interests to have clean air. But if no one else buys a pollution-control device, my having one will not do any good, so I'll just be out the money. On the other hand, if everyone else buys one, then my not having one will not do any harm, so there is no point in my purchasing one." This logic is sound, but if everyone reasoned that way we would never get rid of pollution. Therefore, a *law* is needed to serve the public good.

Here, they say, lies the explanation of why people obey the law. It is not their abstract consent to the actions of a government they have contracted to obey that is in question. Perhaps they did make some such agreement, perhaps not. But their motivation for obeying the law is that the law is, in the long run, for their best interests, too. Law works to make the society better off, to improve the general quality of everyone's environment; therefore we all have a duty to accept it. The social-contract theory goes wrong in its overly formal approach. As far as that theory is concerned, the government can pass any laws it wants as long as the terms of the contract (whatever they may be) are intact. In fact, say the public-interest theorists, service of the common welfare is the only true keystone of the law.

The public-interest theorists thus emphasize that obedience to the law is a social duty. On this point, issue is taken by the "utilitarian" school, who agree that obedience to law is based on what it accomplishes but reject the idea of the public interest as a motivating force. The public-interest theory, like the social contract and traditionalism, is unrealistic because it ignores a basic fact about human nature: selfishness. People obey the law not out of duty to others but from self-interest.

According to the utilitarians, people follow the law for one simple reason: they come out better obeying than disobeying. When a person is faced with a law preventing him from doing something he wishes to do, he asks, "What will happen to me if I violate this law? Will I get caught? What punishment will I receive?" If the danger of being arrested is great and the punishment severe, then people are law-abiding. When enforcement is lax and sentences mild, then we have a crime wave. Everybody supposedly knows this is true. Consequently, when crime rates begin to rise, there is a popular demand for harsher punishments and more police on the beat. Only a few odd legal philosophers call for a revived public interest or a new social contract.

Lawmakers, say the utilitarians, recognize the truth of utilitarian theory. Laws are written to guide people's actions in directions the government believes to be best. By punishing people for engaging in certain activities, the law makes it less in their self-interest to do so, and they refrain. When the law wants people to do something, it makes it in their self-interest to do so by rewarding them (tax deductions for charitable contributions, for instance). This use of rewards and penalties to change people's behavior by changing their self-interest is the whole nature of law.

The utilitarian theory of law, we should observe, tells us nothing about the content of the law, or its purposes. There is an ethical and political philosophy called utilitarianism, which holds that government should seek the greatest happiness for the greatest number of people, and most followers of utilitarian legal theory have accepted this view. However, it is possible to believe in the utilitarian theory of law without bothering about such questions. Self-interest in human nature is the vital element of the theory.

On the other hand, utilitarians have a great deal to say about law enforcement. Since the basis of obedience to law is individual self-interest, laws must be carefully framed to guide people into doing good and avoiding crime, without being two brutal or too expensive. Jeremy Bentham (1748–1832), one of the formulators of utilitarian theory, presented thirteen rules for setting the proper punishment for an offense. Among them:

The cost of punishment should outweigh the benefit of the crime.

The punishment should be no more severe than absolutely necessary.

The less certain it is that the criminal will be caught and punished, the heavier the punishment will have to be.

Since any new law makes the system more complicated, no law should be enacted unless its benefits outweigh this automatic drawback.

In fact, utilitarian thinkers have had a considerable impact on our criminal law and our prison system.

Naturally, the other philosophical theorists are not persuaded by utilitarianism. Just as the utilitarians accuse the other schools of thought of being unrealistic, of ignoring the truth about human behavior, so, too, this charge is leveled against the utilitarians. Utilitarianism, its critics claim, neglects a basic psychological fact: that people believe they have a *duty* to obey the law. Social-contractorians, traditionalists, and public-interest theorists differ on the source of that feeling, but they agree that utilitarianism, with its emphasis on self-interest, cannot explain it at all. Thus, far from being genuinely realistic, they maintain, utilitarianism is little more than a superficial style of cynicism.

Then, What Is Law?

In this welter of theories and approaches, it does not pay to be too hasty in picking sides. Each of these schools of thought has some intelligent adherents, and each has some strong arguments in its favor. Each also has weaknesses. None of them stands out as being clearly superior to the others, as being totally true.

Instead, we find that various ideas are appropriate to various situations and various kinds of law. For example, the historical approach is most helpful when examining the common-law system (Chapter 2). For the study of criminal law, utilitarianism provides useful insights, while realism focuses our attention on the behavior of judges. The rest of this book will consist of varying applications of the many theories of law to the various parts of the law.

And this is really our final answer to the question that opened this chapter: what is law? Law, it turns out, is not one, single thing. It is many-faceted, with numerous people, institutions, and procedures all interacting to deal with human problems and society. From the administrative agency to the Congress, from the justices of the Supreme Court to a tenant signing a lease, law is playing its innumerable roles in our lives. No one can fully define law, and no one can fully understand it; it is too large and too complex to be grasped by any one person. All we can do is select small pieces of the law and look them over one at a time.

2
The Functions
and Types of Law

The most logical way to begin our study of the law is to examine what the law does. In practice, classifying the basic functions of the law is both complicated and controversial: if people cannot agree on what the law is, they are hardly likely to be any more unanimous on how it operates. Any list is bound to be more or less arbitrary. Therefore, arbitrarily, we shall investigate four roles played by the law: (1) prevention and settlement of disputes, (2) enforcement of standards of social behavior, (3) establishment of relations between government and society, and (4) allocation of social resources. In none of these cases, to be sure, does the law act alone, without the involvement of other elements of society. But the law has a large enough share in each of these duties to make them worth looking into.

To Prevent and Settle Disputes

It is a common practice to consult with an attorney before making certain decisions, to ascertain if "the law" will per-

mit proposed actions. Lawyers certainly stress the importance of securing legal counsel in a timely fashion in order
to prevent a "lawsuit." (The problem of securing and paying an attorney will be discussed in Chapter 4.) Merely
because one sees an attorney does not mean that the ensuing advice will keep one out of court, however. After all,
laws are like many other things: they are subject to various
interpretations by various people. Two lawyers may disagree over the meaning of a contract provision just as easily
as two doctors might disagree over the diagnosis and treatment of a patient. Nevertheless, once the law has been interpreted and applied, it will provide the basis for resolving conflict; and this interpretation might very well be
used by lawyers and judges in similar situations to aid
them in preventing or settling other disputes. Thus, the
law may be used to keep people out of the judicial arena
by delineating their legal relationships, or when necessary,
to provide a means of adjudicating their dispute.

Let us examine a hypothetical case that may help us understand this particular function of law. North and South
are neighbors; for years, they have been sharing a common
driveway, which is situated between their two properties.
They have also shared the expenses of maintaining the
driveway. Then, one day, North and South have an argument: North claims he owns the entire driveway; South
makes the same claim for himself.

At this point we have a dispute between North and
South over ownership of the driveway. It is quite possible
that society's legal institutions will not be used to settle
North and South's disagreement. North and South may
work out a compromise of some kind. Perhaps neighbors
East and West will bring the competing parties together
to resolve their differences. The wives of the two individuals may bring pressure to bear on both men to settle the
dispute.

If none of these methods enables North and South to
reach agreement, then they may consult their lawyers. The

attorneys may both come to the same conclusion, that North has "title" to the driveway (that is, he owns it and can sell it), but South has an "easement" (he has a legal right to use the driveway). On the other hand, the two lawyers might disagree, in which case North and South might go to court and let a judge settle their dispute. Even a court verdict might be insufficient, and one or both of the people might take the case to a higher court (this is called an "appeal"). Other variations could also result.

This single boundary dispute could develop into something more complicated, resulting in the need for society, through its legal institutions, to compel—by various means—compliance with the law by the parties involved. For example, assume that North is ordered by the court to allow South the use of the driveway. North ignores the court and erects a barricade at the drive entrance, forcing South to enlist the aid of the court in compelling North to abide by its decision. Instead of going to court, South, not a patient person, uses his car as a tank and plows through the barricade erected by North; this action would set off another "legal chain reaction" as society attempts to settle a dispute involving two of its members.

To Enforce Standards of Social Behavior

If one were to drive a car at sixty-five miles per hour through a city street, fail to pay taxes due, ignore a subpoena, or sneak into a circus without paying, chances are he would come into contact with law-enforcement agencies established and maintained by society. If, however, an individual were to smoke an excessive number of cigarettes, write a letter to a newspaper or magazine denouncing the President's economic policies, or join the Ku Klux Klan or the Communist Party, such actions would not result in society's imposing penalties through its legal institutions. Other institutions, e.g. the family, might attempt some form of control over such conduct, however.

The dilemma presented here is as old as society itself: What social behavior shall be restricted? and how? and when? Our concern here is with the control of human behavior by society through its legal institutions and with the point at which the authority of an organized society is to be used to enforce standards of social behavior, "the end result being," in the words of sociologist Max Weber (1864–1920), "conformity or to avenge a violation." That is, certain individual actions are viewed by society as being in need of regulation through its system of law and legal procedures, while other actions do not require supervision.

At what point the authority of society will become involved with certain kinds of human behavior is dependent upon a number of factors. The complexity of society and its mores, folkways, and taboos are important considerations. For example, the relatively simple society of the Eskimos needs rely only on community action, while in our society we must rely on a central authority with a monopoly on force for the enforcement of standards of social behavior.

In the North-South controversy, there never would have been a dispute in the first place, in some societies, since all land is communally owned. But where this is not the case, the relationship between North and South and their conduct in the conflict would be influenced by standards of behavior established by society, by formal control—law—and/or by informal pressure, i.e. other social controls. We place great emphasis on the institution of private property within our society. As such, we find the law extensively involved when it comes to property relationships, producing early involvement by central authority, as was the case in the North-South argument over property. What we are suggesting is a general theme of conflict resolution and social behavior within our society; there are many variations on the theme. Would North and South's behavior, for example, be influenced by the fact that North was the community's police chief? That the dispute occurred in Boston, Massachusetts, or Tonkawa, Oklahoma? That South was employed by North?

Law, however, is only as effective as people's response to it. We have already seen that philosophers offer differing explanations of why people obey the law. If we move from the philosophers to the people themselves, we get an equally wide variety of answers. Sometimes, people support a law because they support an individual involved in a dispute. Others believe the law is generally socially beneficial, whatever the circumstances of a single case. Still others feel that compliance is the right thing, regardless of their views of the value of the law or the intelligence of the lawmakers. Whatever the reason, obedience usually helps to sustain a social order beneficial to them all.

Unfortunately, governments can use the goal of protecting the social order to justify laws that work only to protect the privileges of those in power. Most Americans would agree, for instance, that suppression of unpopular ideas or censorship of the press is not needed for society to operate; indeed, many would insist that the right to express one's opinions results in the system's working better. At the same time, everyone agrees that there must be some limits on personal activities. Holding a protest demonstration against school busing is one thing; bombing school buses is something else.

The boundary is far from clear. In practice, if a large segment of society, especially a majority, feel strongly that a law is wrong, then the law will probably not work, no matter how useful to the social order it might be. A classic example was Prohibition, which forebade ". . . the manufacture, sale, or transportation of intoxicating liquors within, the importation thereof into, or the exportation thereof from the United States . . . for beverage purposes

. . ." (the last clause meant that liquor could be used for medicine with a doctor's prescription). Many people who opposed the law obeyed it anyway, but enough people did not to make the whole affair a disaster.

To Establish Relations Between Government and Society

In the United States, the Constitution establishes the framework within which the government and the people interact. The Constitution grants the government certain powers; e.g., "The Congress shall have power . . . [t]o lay and collect taxes. . . ." (How well we know!) The Constitution also restricts the government; e.g., "Congress shall make no law respecting an establishment of religion, or prohibiting the free exercise thereof. . . ." Not all societies have such written documents to spell out the relations between persons and states, and many countries that do possess such official constitutions ignore them. One way or another, though, every system must deal with the problem of the rights and duties of citizens vis-à-vis their regime.

A written constitution is certainly a convenience, since it delineates rules more clearly than unwritten custom or tradition, and numerous countries have adopted the American practice of a set of fundamental principles to regulate their systems. However, even a written document leaves considerable room for interpretation and growth. Take, for example, one apparently straightforward concept: "due process of law." In our system, as in most Western democracies, government's regulation of citizen behavior must be guided by due process of law, and not be arbitrary or irrational. The meaning of the term, though, has changed and developed over the centuries.

No one really knows just when the concept of due process of law first originated. Its earliest well-known appearance came in the Magna Charta, a document that granted civil and political rights to some classes in England. (Several artists have portrayed the stirring historic moment in 1215 when King John signed the Magna Charta at Runnymede. In reality, these pictures are more stirring than historic; King John was illiterate.) In the Magna Charta, the term "law of the land" was used, and this eventually developed into "due process of law."

The United States Constitution refers to due process of law twice. In the Fifth Amendment it says, ". . . nor shall any person be . . . deprived of life, liberty, or property, without due process of law. . . ." The Fourteenth Amendment reads identically except that it begins ". . . nor shall any State deprive. . . ." The Fourteenth Amendment, which was added to the Constitution in 1868, was required because the Supreme Court had ruled that the Fifth Amendment, and the entire Bill of Rights (Amendments I to X) applied only to relations between citizens and the federal government, so some regulation of state governments was needed. In fact, the Supreme Court in the twentieth century has used the Fourteenth Amendment and the due-process clause as a device to extend provisions of the Bill of Rights to the states. Due process of law, then, means different things in the two amendments. In the Fifth, it refers simply to legal procedure; while in the Fourteenth, it encompasses a large number of personal and political freedoms.

Not all personal and political freedoms, though. Despite efforts by some of its justices (Supreme Court justices disagree as much as any other set of lawyers—or politicians), the court has never accepted the proposition that the entire Bill of Rights is incorporated into the Fourteenth Amendment. Rather, it has followed a practice called "selective absorption," applying some provisions of the Bill of Rights to the states (freedom of speech, right to an attorney) but not others (right to a twelve-person jury and unanimous verdict in criminal trials, right to a grand-jury indictment before prosecution). This selection process has been going on since 1925 (some historians date it back to the end of the nineteenth century) and has provided much scope for lawsuits and for confusion.

The complexity of the situation is compounded by the fact that there are two kinds of due process within the Fourteenth Amendment itself: "procedural" and "substantive." Procedural due process refers to the *methods* the government uses in dealing with members of society. For procedural due process, what counts is not the results of government actions but how government achieves its ends. In our society, there are certain means the government simply cannot use and get away with. For instance, in one case the police illegally entered a man's home, saw him swallowing what they thought were drugs, and proceeded to get hold of the evidence first by wrestling him to the floor and sticking their fingers down his throat and second by handcuffing him and taking him to a hospital, where his stomach was pumped. They retrieved the drug capsules, and the man was convicted, but the Supreme Court unanimously reversed the conviction. Some things the government cannot do, even to prevent crime. Further, if such conduct were allowed, next time the police might make a mistake and treat an innocent person that way. Such behavior violates due process of law.

Substantive due process deals with the *content* of the law. Sometimes, even when the government adopts correct procedures, the results it comes up with are so outrageous and unfair that they should not be enforced. Especially in the 1920s and 1930s, the Supreme Court declared many laws unconstitutional on these grounds, particularly the economic legislation of Roosevelt's New Deal. These decisions were widely unpopular, and in 1937 the court shifted its approach. Since then, few if any economic laws have been held to violate substantive due process. The concept, instead, has been redirected in recent times to family and consumer affairs, such as abortion and installment buying.

The concept of due process and the nature of proper relations between society and government is a vexed question in American law. Other countries, although they lack a Fifth or a Fourteenth Amendment, still face the same basic problems. As each case presents itself, judges and citizens must again ask themselves the query posed by Justice Benjamin Cardozo (1870–1938) in 1937:

[Is it] a hardship so acute and shocking that our polity will not endure it? Does it violate those "fundamental principles of liberty and justice which lie at the base of all our civil and political institutions" . . . [and] which are implicit in the concept of ordered liberty . . . [or] violate a principle of justice, so rooted in the traditions and conscience of our people as to be ranked as fundamental?

To Allocate Social Resources

Professional economists often maintain that it is the function of the market to allocate resources in a society; one well-known definition of politics is the "authoritative allocation of values." Without denying the significance of either economics or politics, though, we cannot fully understand the distribution of goods and services in a society without also examining its legal system.

The law is involved in the allocation of resources in two ways. First, the law regulates private action. Even the most fervent believer in the free enterprise system and laissez faire does not want to extend economic freedom to bank robbers and hijackers (although some adherents of the radical theory of law might disagree). When it comes to dividing up the benefits of society, especially its material goods, we prefer to give individuals as much latitude as possible in choosing for themselves what they want and what they will do to get it, but some methods must be forbidden. Law allows freedom but prohibits force and fraud.

This aspect of the law seems relatively uncontroversial:

few people publicly advocate a larger role for muggers and forgers in our society. As we might expect, however, matters become less clear-cut when we get down to cases. For instance, everyone can agree that it is improper to force someone to sign a contract at gunpoint, as such actions are illegal all over the world. But what do we do about the fast-talking door-to-door salesperson who high-pressures someone into purchasing some item he can neither use nor afford? Until recently, the law stayed out of this type of exchange, but now a customer is entitled to a "cooling off" period before the agreement is binding. Such sales do not exactly involve force or fraud, but society feels that they require regulation nonetheless.

Regulation of private action insofar as it involves the distribution of wealth dominates a large part of law. Most contract law, for instance (Chapter 5), concerns itself with supervising private economic activities. In addition, much criminal law deals with legitimate and illegitimate means of acquiring goods. Lawyers concentrating in corporate law tend, naturally enough, to make the most money, which guarantees that the field will not be neglected. Still, legal participation in the allocation of resources is not restricted to this supervision. Law also directly parcels out shares in social benefits.

Taxes are the most obvious form of legal allocation of resources. Essentially, a tax is a law that separates people from some of their money and places it at the disposal of the government. Instead of letting individuals decide for themselves how they will spend their incomes, the government makes the decision for them. Law determines who will pay what, when, and how, and who will receive. Needless to say, law and lawmakers have shown substantial ingenuity in regulating both the paying and the receiving ends.

Taxes may be classified in various ways: by what they tax, how they are paid, who pays how much. There are taxes on property, on sales, on incomes, on imports, on luxuries, and on almost anything else one can imagine. When people pay the government themselves (as with income taxes), the tax is called a "direct" tax. With an "indirect" tax (e.g. sales tax), the people pay their money to a middleman, who in turn passes it on to the government. Politicians prefer indirect taxes, all else being equal, because voters are less likely to notice them and take it out on the incumbents at the next election. Also significant is the difference between "progressive" and "regressive" taxes. If persons with more money pay a larger percentage of their money for the tax than poorer people, the tax is termed progressive. A sales tax is usually regressive, since wealthy people spend proportionately less of their incomes on the tax. Clearly, taxation is an area where law, economics, and politics intermingle freely.

Governments have found as many ways to spend money as they have to collect it. A law may be required to provide a benefit for the community as a whole that no individual person might be able or willing to pay for alone. As the public-interest theory of law points out (Chapter 1), a policy that may be good for everyone may not be in the self-interest of anyone. We may all agree that we need an army for national defense, but no one is going to buy one at the supermarket. We need a law.

Law gets involved in the direct allocation of resources also when the results of private efforts strike the society as unfair or unacceptable. For example, most of us agree that small children should not go hungry because their parents are poor, so the law provides aid to dependent children. But such aid is not limited entirely, or even mostly, to the poor. During the nineteenth century, the government decided it was vital for our growth that railroads be built across the country. The Congress proceeded to pass a law granting economic benefits and subsidies to the railroad companies to encourage their development. Government money has gone to farmers, to aircraft corporations, and to universities, among others. (Laws can also benefit one element in society by taxing another; for example, tariffs on imported automobiles are an indirect subsidy to domestic car manufacturers.) Here again, it is hard to decide whether we are discussing law, economics, or politics.

The discussion has indicated that the four functions of law are not very markedly distinct: if resources are not allocated well, social disorder may result; enforcing acceptable standards of social behavior helps prevent disputes, and preventing disputes, in turn, maintains social order; settling quarrels between individual citizens and the government entails both controlling the government and resolving conflict; and so on. In studying law, categories are useful conveniences to sort out and arrange phenomena, but we must never forget that laws are not written to fall into neat classifications and pigeonholes. Distinctions are valuable only when they are not taken too seriously.

Types of Law

Having warned against the perils of categories, we shall now proceed to review the traditional divisions made among the varieties of American law. We begin by distinguishing between "private" and "public" law. Private law is concerned with the relationships between individuals; its major thrust is to establish the legal relationships among members of society. Since there are many members and relationships, there are correspondingly many subdivisions in private law. Among the major groupings are (1) the "contract"—an agreement between persons that establishes, modifies, or terminates a legal relation (see Chapter 5); (2) "torts"—civil wrongs committed against a person or property, excluding matters of contract (and also excluding *criminal* wrongs, which fall under public law), e.g. auto accidents; (3) "property"—which concerns the free use of a person's acquisitions except in those situations in which use is restricted by appropriate laws, e.g.

zoning regulations (see Chapter 6—the dispute between North and South, discussed earlier, was a matter of property law); and (4) "corporate law"—dealing essentially with a legal entity, usually a business or charity, created under the authority of state or national laws.

Relationships among members of our complex society are usually not simple, and our laws reflect this fact. As we shall see, the act of purchasing something or renting a place in which to live may be a complicated undertaking. Dying may be on many occasions an uncomplicated act and an end in many ways, but it is really only the beginning in other respects. Should Forgetful Flangswister suddenly be called to glory and leave a million dollars but no will (that is, he dies "intestate"), what happens to the million dollars? All kinds of grieving relatives may make an appearance (as will the federal government and the state) to lay claim to portions of the estate. The law of the appropriate state (and even which state might be in controversy) would be used to determine who is to get what share of the estate. When the deceased is both wealthy and famous, like Pablo Picasso or Howard Hughes, the ensuing litigation can keep both lawyers and newspapers in business for years. If society had no law to deal with situations of this kind, every death would bring on comparable, if less extravagant, complications.

Public law affects and is applicable to society as a whole. That is, it is the public—society in a collective sense —that falls under the scope and purpose of public law. Such law not only concerns the relationship between individuals and the state but the government itself. Unlike as in private law, the state may very well be a party in a public lawsuit, e.g. *The People of New Jersey* v. *O'Hara*. The principal objective of public law is to deal with those social matters that pertain to the well-being of society—the public. Laws dealing with regulation of the environment fall into this category. So does a state law establishing and maintaining a social welfare program. One that could relate to our North-South dispute would be a local zoning law. Suppose South decides to give up his claim of ownership of the driveway and elects to get even by converting his home into an all-night restaurant. Think of all the traffic—vehicular and pedestrian! the cooking odors (South aims all the kitchen exhaust toward North's house!) the bright neon light flashing SOUTH'S SOUP AND SAN' SHOP off and on day and night! Naturally, society cannot permit its members to use their property in such a fashion. It is not just North who would be harmed by such tactics; society as a whole would face possible calamity if such practices were allowed.

One important branch of public law is "constitutional law," which deals with the constitutions of the United States and the fifty states. A constitution is the fundamental law of a political body. It creates the structure of government, and both grants and limits governmental authority. Any law or action in conflict with a constitution is null and void. In our federal system, the national Constitution is "the supreme law of the land," which means that any state law, action, or even constitutional provision in conflict with the national Constitution is unconstitutional and invalid.

The national Constitution (ratified in 1788) and all the state constitutions are written documents, although, as we have mentioned, not all societies operate this way. The British constitution, for instance, is unwritten, which means it is impossible to obtain a copy of it, for no such paper exists. Rather, their constitution is a collection of major parliamentary laws, judicial decisions, traditions, and customs. Since any act of Parliament is thus technically constitutional, there is no judicial body in Great Britain that has the authority to annul a national law. The British constitution is enforced politically instead, as the British have a strong sense of what is or is not in the "spirit" of the constitution.

Examining some American constitutions may help explain the British preference for unwritten rules. For its part, the federal Constitution is a well-crafted document. It is about eight thousand words long, and has been amended only twenty-six times in almost two centuries (less, really, since the first ten amendments—the Bill of Rights—were almost part of the original Constitution). State constitutions are another matter altogether. They average thirty-two thousand words, ranging from five to seven thousand (Vermont, Connecticut and Rhode Island) to six hundred thousand (Georgia). The states are also more liberal with their amendments; e.g., California's constitution has over 350 amendments. Moreover, most of the states have discarded one or two constitutions over the years and instituted new ones.

The national Constitution deals less with details; it also reflects a broad outline of governmental structures and functions; states, on the other hand, have residual powers (Tenth Amendment) and consequently require more detail in their charters. Indeed, these documents have often been cluttered up with some remarkable trivia, primarily as a result of interest groups' wanting to encase their interests in the state's supreme law, and some strange notions about what is "fundamental." For example, California's constitution restricts the legislature's power in establishing time limits on wrestling matches.

The differences between written and unwritten constitutions should not be exaggerated, however. Our national Constitution has undergone several significant changes even without amendments. Judicial interpretation has been one method of effecting innovations in the authority of Congress, the President, the states, and the judiciary itself, as the brief history of the due-process clause showed. Also, the United States has produced important customs of its own not mentioned in the Constitution, such as political parties. Written or unwritten, the essence of constitutionalism remains the same: to limit government to actions in some way authorized by the people it governs.

Common Law

American law has been and continues to be influenced by "common law." This law is characterized as being unwritten because it is not based on formally enacted legislation; it is the result of judicial decisions. It is written, however, to the extent that many of the judges' decisions have been recorded and have been reflected in or have affected decisions in other cases.

King Henry II of England (1133–89), the first of the Plantagenets, established a rudimentary judicial system in his country. As this system expanded and developed, the common law (probably so called to distinguish it from law found in the ecclesiastical courts) began to emerge from the king's courts. The king's judges would "ride the circuit," that is, travel around an assigned area to hear disputes and charges. They would attempt to apply the appropriate principles of law to the facts in a consistent manner. Where the facts presented could not be handled by such a principle, then the judge would create one. While on circuit, the judges would seek overnight accommodations at local inns, where they would share and exchange experiences and judicial opinions. These exchanges were then used by fellow judges when judging similar cases, which helped to some degree in developing consistency of opinions in like cases. Further, summaries of many court proceedings found their way into what were termed *Year Books*.

Sir Edward Coke (pronounced "Cook") (1552–1634), one of England's most noted jurists, culled and analyzed many cases and established legal maxims and rules based on his analyses. Another English jurist, Sir William Blackstone (1723–80), enlarged upon and clarified the works of Coke in his famous *Commentaries on the Laws of England*, which formed the foundation for legal training in eighteenth- and nineteenth-century Britain. In the United States, Blackstone's work was supplemented by commentaries by New York Chancellor James Kent (1763–1847) and Supreme Court Justice Joseph Story (1779–1845). It has remained a distinguishing mark of the common-law tradition that commentators, as well as judges, exert important shaping influences.

The basis of the common-law tradition is the development of principles based on a series of individual cases. A judge faced with a novel problem attempts to resolve it in a reasoned opinion. Encountering a similar problem, later courts examine the argument that the first judge used to justify his decision. If they find it sound, they will apply the same line of reasoning to their own cases. More often, they find some merit in the earlier proceedings but see a need to rework and modify the analysis. Other courts build on this new approach, and so a principle is shaped, to become a part of common law.

Common law thus gives considerable discretion to individual judges. This freedom is enhanced by the doctrine of judicial creativity, a concept analyzed most fully by Justice Cardozo. In Cardozo's view, the actions of earlier courts were only points of departure for future decisions. Judges have four methods at their disposal to deal with new situations. First, they can extend the principles of previous cases to their logical conclusions. Second, they can extend previous principles in the direction indicated by the historical background of prior decisions. Third, they can adhere to well-established custom in the community. These approaches are relatively straightforward and require little creativity. However, when none of these methods seems appropriate, judges can give freer rein to their own insights. Acknowledging the changing needs of modern society, judges seek to maintain the *spirit* of earlier decisions while modifying the principles, to meet the new social and economic realities and still achieve justice. This fourth tool fosters growth and change in common law.

In the opposition to judicial creativity stands the doctrine of *"stare decisis."* This term refers to the rule that courts follow precedents, that they do just what earlier courts did. Adherence to *stare decisis* ensures stability. It guarantees to persons in the society that courts will act in predictable ways. Moreover, *stare decisis* makes life easier for judges too, especially inexperienced ones. As long as they need only follow precedents, judges will not be obliged to rely solely on their own personal wisdom in each case they handle. *Stare decisis,* finally, serves as a limit on judicial power and helps prevent arbitrary decisions.

Stare decisis is only one of several factors in common law that enhances stability. One specialist, Professor Karl Llewellyn (1893–1962), has detailed no fewer than fourteen such elements. Among the more important:

Judges are "law-conditioned"; their whole training and experience teaches them to rely on previous decisions.

Common law provides such a large reservoir of principles that innovation is seldom necessary.

Judges are required to write "opinions," official statements of the reasons for their decisions. Unjustified changes are hard to defend.

The issues courts face are constantly narrowed and refined, so that only reasonably clear questions are presented for judicial decision.

Generally, appellate courts (see Chapter 3), which make the most influential decisions, include several members, who balance each other.

The traditions of judicial honesty and independence keep most judges from yielding to pressure groups or popular fashions.

Finally, judges have a self-image of professionalism. They want to win the esteem of their fellow professionals, both on courts and in law schools. They want to uphold standards of judicial craftsmanship. While this self-image, and all these points together, do not prevent all change, they do tend to impede wild swings from one principle to another and to discourage unnecessary forays into uncharted legal areas.

Originally, the major focal point of common law was "real property": land and that which is permanently fixed or growing on it. Other areas were gradually added, such as criminal matters, torts, and contracts. The thrust of common law continues to be in these areas, with the exception of criminal law, in which statutory provisions have assumed a dominant role.

An example of a common-law crime would be burglary. This act was made a crime as a result of some judicial decision (and reinforced by subsequent decisions) way back in English history. If someone in England broke and entered, in the wording of the common law, "in the night time, into the dwelling house of another with the intent to commit a felony therein," then that person was guilty of a crime, burglary. Clearly, the judge ruling on a case in which one was accused of this criminal act would want to know a number of things; for example, what does it mean to "break"? to "enter"? When is it "night time"? What is meant by "intent"? If the accused broke and entered in the daytime, then could he be guilty of burglary? If not, would the law then permit breaking, entering, and a felonious act? Hardly. A judge could rule, based upon judicial reasoning and common sense, that some other antisocial act has been committed and the act would become a common-law crime. A common-law marriage would be an example of a civil matter in the area of the common law. Again, judicial decisions developed the "law" that a man and woman living together as man and wife for a period of time, say seven years, would be considered legally husband and wife. This is still the rule in some states; many states have enacted laws abolishing common-law marriages, making a civil or religious ceremony necessary before man and woman are legally wedded.

Over the centuries, the common-law system was modified by the development of other types of law, especially equity and statutory legislation. Before we discuss these modifications, we shall contrast common law to the system prevalent in continental Europe, the "civil-law system."

Civil-law System

In the sixth century the Byzantine Emperor Justinian I ordered his jurists to codify the Roman law, which had governed the great Roman Empire. The outcome was a collection of twelve books, which the emperor summarized in three main points: live honestly, hurt no one, and give everyone his due. Needless to say, this abridged version omitted some important details, and legal scholars of the empire preferred to utilize the more complete edition, which became known as the Justinian Code, or simply The Code. The Code stood as the basis for European law until the time of Napoleon. This new emperor, recognizing that the Justinian Code was very much out of date, and hoping that a new code would add to his prestige and serve as a legal system for a united Europe (under his rule, of course), promulgated a modernized code in 1804. This Code Napoléon (Napoleonic Code), or Code Civil, has played a most important part in modern continental European legal systems and areas under their influence (such as the Middle East and, in the United States, the former French colony of Louisiana).

Civil law, then, is basically statutory in form, a collection and codification of official rules. In contrast, common law builds on a case-by-case basis, following the rule of *stare decisis*, and deciding cases the way previous judges decided them (this procedure is also known as "following precedents"). To be sure, common-law countries do have written law codes, and civil-law countries do have precedents, but the difference in emphasis is quite important.

Equity

Ironically, it was the developing standardization of the common-law system which underlined its major deficiency, a lack of flexibility. For example, if someone negligently damaged a landowner's property, the owner could collect payment. The owner, however, might be far more interested in *preventing* the damage from occurring in the first place, but here the common law was no help. A building contractor decides to develop a subdivision of a hundred lots and buys enough acreage to do so. At the last minute, though, the owner of a small section of the whole area changes his mind and refuses to sell. Under the common law, the seller has breached his contract and the contractor can sue him for compensation, but the contractor does not want compensation; he wants the section, to fill out his subdivision. In any case, simply getting his money back would hardly compensate him for the expenses connected with the now-defunct development. Some other remedy is definitely necessary.

As a result of this inflexibility in the common law, "equity" (or rules of "chancery") developed in England in the fourteenth century, when the king's chancellor (who acted for the king and based his decisions on the king's wishes) began to hear grievances from citizens who could not, for some reason, find justice in the common-law courts. This arrangement grew into a separate court, most rapidly during the sixteenth century, when requests to the chancellor for justice—"let right be done"—began to increase. A dual court system ensued, with law (common law) and equity (or chancery). Suits in the former were termed "action at law," while proceedings in the latter were referred to as an "equitable remedy." This arrangement, of courts of law and courts of equity (or chancery courts), was also implemented in the colonies and carried over into the American legal system. Most states have abolished this dual system, and judges today hear both types of suits in their courts.

Although common law and equity have merged, some important differences remain. Equity, for instance, offers remedies to the person bringing suit not available in (common) law. Under common law, the contractor could re-

ceive only "damages" from the landowner, that is, monetary compensation for his loss. Using his equity power,
however, a judge can order "specific performance," that is,
he can insist that the owner of the plot of land go through
with the promised sale. The advantage of this device is obvious.

Equity offers other instruments not present in law.
Under equity, a judge can issue an "injunction," a decree
requiring or forbidding a specific action, or an "involuntary trust," which compels a person who has defrauded
someone else to correct the fraud by acting in the victim's
interests. A judge's power to hold someone in "contempt
of court" when he has refused to obey a court order or has
affronted the court's dignity (cursed the judge, etc.) also
derives from equity. Using the contempt power, a judge
can fine or even imprison an individual.

Choosing to make use of the procedures and remedies
of equity also involves disadvantages and restrictions for
the individual bringing suit. Equity power will not be employed if money damages are sufficient for compensation.
Again, equity permits certain defenses not recognized in
common law. If the contractor develops another subdivision, and only later sues in court for specific performance by the landowner, the seller can argue that it is too
late for this remedy because the contractor, by his omission or negligence, has abandoned his right or claim (a defense called "laches"). Equity also permits the judge great
discretion, including authority to refuse to act at all (not
so when money damages are sought). Finally, in equity
there is no right to jury trial.

How does one know whether something is "law" or "equity"? The answer depends on a number of things, such as
the facts involved, the remedy sought, etc. But the years
have seen the expression of principles of equity in
"maxims." There is no definitive list of these maxims, but
a few will give some idea of how equity operates: "He
who seeks equity must do equity." "He who comes into

equity must come with clean hands." "Equity imposes an interest to fill an obligation." "Equity abhors a forfeiture." "Equity will not suffer a wrong to be without a remedy." "Equity delights to do justice and not by halves."

Statutory Law

Statutory law is law that has been formally written and adopted by one of the lawmaking bodies of society. These bodies include Congress, state legislatures, city councils, administrative agencies, and numerous others (for a full discussion, see Chapters 6, 7, and 8). In short, statutory law is what the legal positivists have in mind when they speak of law, or what law means in the Code Civil.

For present purposes, the important thing to note about statutory law is that it supersedes common law whenever there is any conflict between the two. Thus, the common-law definition of burglary is no longer applicable anywhere in the United States, as all the states have enacted statutes regarding burglary. Ohio, for example, distinguishes among "aggravated burglary" (trespass in an occupied building, intending to rob or commit a felony, and somehow raising the threat of harm to anyone, e.g. by carrying a weapon), "burglary" (trespass to commit a felony), and "breaking and entering" (trespassing in an unoccupied building with intent to commit a felony), each a less serious crime than the one before. Of course, these distinctions were not invented by the Ohio legislature, but their legal status is based on the legislature's authority and not, as in common law, on judge-made precedent.

Civil Law and Criminal Law

The term "civil law," when used in the American legal system, does not usually refer to the European Code Civil, but to the law concerned with personal relationships and interests (hence it overlaps to a large extent with private law). On the whole, the law prefers to remain outside of private affairs. It does establish rules for such relationships, and procedures and penalties to be invoked if the rules are violated. Beyond this point, however, the law restricts itself to providing a judicial arena in which private parties can resolve their disputes. Even when the government is involved in a civil suit, its role is limited to that of just another party.

Civil law can involve statutory law, or it may entail common law or equity. Its distinguishing feature is that the full responsibility for invoking it rests on the people involved in the disagreement. They go to court, they prepare and argue the case (or, rather, pay attorneys to do it for them), they request certain compensation or judgment, they gather the evidence. According to the theory of civil law, individuals and not society have been injured, so it is the individuals who are responsible for seeking redress.

Civil law, therefore, contrasts strongly with "criminal law," which is concerned with acts or offenses against the public, the society as a whole. Consequently, society (or its representative) brings the case against the alleged violator of the law, and the criminal law itself sets the appropriate penalty. The theory of criminal law is that certain actions not only harm individuals, they make the world a worse place for everybody. Murder, arson, rape, embezzlement, and so on tend to disrupt the equilibrium of a country and destroy the common good. To prevent this disruption, societies have erected large criminal-justice systems to locate and punish offenders. If the system runs efficiently and fairly (with due process of law), the social peace will presumably be better preserved.

A single act can fall under both civil and criminal law. For instance, if an irate shoe salesman begins beating a customer over the head with a shoe, the police will intervene and prosecute the salesman for "assault and battery," which is a criminal offense. However, the customer may also go to court and sue the salesman for the injuries he inflicted. The customer's suit is a *civil* suit, as he is seeking damages for a personal injury. The district attorney is arguing a *criminal* case, because of a crime against society as a whole.

Criminal law is almost entirely statutory, although it did originate in common law. For the most part, crimes are divided into two types, "felonies" and "misdemeanors." A felony (the common law called felonies "true crimes") is a major criminal act usually punishable by a prison term of a year or more—up to the death penalty—and a possible fine. A misdemeanor is a minor criminal act that usually results in a jail sentence of less than a year (in a local jail) and a small fine. The distinction between the two is based on the punishment, not the offense, since what may be a felony in one state may be a misdemeanor in another.

Some punishable offenses are not classified as crimes at all. Instead, they are labeled "petty offenses" and are handled in brief hearings called "summary proceedings." The dividing line between the petty non-criminal offense and the minor criminal misdemeanor is far from clear. For instance, public intoxication is a misdemeanor in some states and a petty offense in others. Moreover, many jurisdictions in the United States use "violation" as the term to describe offenses less serious than misdemeanors. In some states, a violation is defined as something other than a traffic infraction (which is a petty offense), with a maximum sentence of fifteen days. The terminology, though, is not uniform.

Other Types of Law

There is no end to the types of law that exist in the United States, and no effort will be made here to cover all the ones that remain. One or two, however, deserve some special note.

"Administrative law" is the branch of statutory law

produced by the numerous special agencies that have mushroomed in the United States in the twentieth century. These bodies, established by legislatures or by state constitutions, are not exactly legislative, executive, or judicial in nature, but combine all three duties. They are unique in that they not only make rules, they also both prosecute and try alleged violators of their own regulations. Although the regular courts often distrust these commissions, and a court may intervene if it believes the agencies are acting unfairly, the specialized expertise of the bodies gives them great leeway. How adequately they work will be taken up in Chapter 8.

The United States Constitution also provides for a special law of the seas. Article III, Section 2, of the Constitution says that "all cases of admiralty and maritime jurisdiction" shall rest in the federal judicial system. "Admiralty law" is concerned with acts committed on the seas or upon navigable waters of the United States ("navigable waters" include any body of water that could, by reasonable improvement, be made navigable). The determining factor is the location. For "maritime law," the key issue is subject matter; it focuses on commercial transactions related to shipping, such as shippers' contracts or maritime insurance rates.

On one side, admiralty and maritime law interacts with state laws. The states may adopt legislation creating rights enforceable in federal court cases of an admiralty-maritime nature as long as the laws do not disturb the unity of maritime law that the Constitution sought to establish, a matter the courts must determine. Further, the states do have the power to enforce their local laws on navigable waters (e.g., a homicide on a private boat in Chesapeake Bay).

On the other side, maritime law often intersects "international law," the law of nations. International law has a long and honorable history, dating back in its modern form to a Dutch jurist named Hugo Grotius (1583–1645). Nonetheless, its legal status has always been questionable.

The problem with international law is that there is no international government with the power and responsibility to enforce it. To be sure, for the past half century or so there has been an international court, but it has no way of enforcing its decisions on anyone, or even of compelling a party to appear before it. International law is itself divided up in various ways—law of war and law of peace, private international law and public international law—but its most characteristic feature is that it is formed largely by treaties, i.e. by voluntary agreements among states (like contracts, but without courts to enforce penalties or compensation). Despite its problematic status as genuine law, international law has grown in importance as the nations of the world have grown more and more interdependent.

3
The Court System

The structure of our country's judicial system is dualistic. As a part of our federal system, we have two sets of courts, one operated by the national government and another run at the state level by each of the state governments. Both of these judicial networks are extensive; at times they conflict. The nature of American law cannot be understood without an examination of both types of courts.

The dual court system goes back to the Constitution itself, which left existing state court systems intact, established the Supreme Court, and gave Congress the authority "To constitute tribunals inferior to the Supreme Court." Shortly after the Constitution was adopted, Congress exercised its power in the Judiciary Act of 1789, which laid down the lines for our present court organization by creating federal "District Courts" to hear cases concerning federal laws, and "Circuit Courts" to hear appeals from district-court decisions.

There are other ways to build judicial systems. For instance, Canada also has a federal structure, with a central government and ten provinces. Moreover, criminal law in Canada is largely federal (in the United States it is mostly state law). The principal trial and appellate (appeals) work, however, is handled by provincial courts applying federal law. Except for the Canadian Supreme Court, all the federal courts are specialized: Tax Review, Immigration, and so on. Conflicts between the two systems are not nearly as common as in the United States.

The tension in the American approach grows from the fact that federal courts are not necessarily superior to state courts. A federal court cannot order a state court to do something just because it is federal. Before any federal court, including the Supreme Court, can supersede an action by a state court, it must show that there is a federal issue involved. If not, no federal court can intervene. State courts, naturally, strongly support this rule. The problem is that it is up to the federal courts to decide what a federal issue is, and they take a broader view of the matter than the state judges would like. This expansion of the role of the federal courts, of course, is only one part of a more general expansion of the role of the national government in the past half century.

Article III of the Constitution provides the basic definition of a federal issue, using two tests: the subject matter of the case, and the parties involved in the dispute. There are three subject matters that fall in the "jurisdiction" of the federal courts, i.e. that are argued before federal judges: cases arising under the Constitution, cases arising under federal laws or treaties, and admiralty or maritime cases (see Chapter 2). In these instances, federal courts take charge because the dispute centers on some regulation or rule of the national government. Assigning cases to federal courts is also done when there is a need for judges who would, most likely, be more impartial arbiters than state judges: cases involving foreign ambassadors, ministers or consuls; cases in which the United States Government is a party; controversies between two or more states; controversies, involving ten thousand dollars or more, between citizens of different states; disputes between a state (or its citizens) and a foreign country (or its citizens); and controversies between citizens of the same state claiming lands under grants from different states (now obsolete). In a 1793 case the Supreme Court had ruled that federal jurisdiction also extended to a case in which a citizen of one state sued another state, but this decision was reversed by the Eleventh Amendment, and such cases are now tried in the courts of the state being sued.

Most of these principles are straightforward enough, but there is a complicating factor in cases in which the United States is a party. Under a doctrine called "sovereign immunity," no one can sue the government unless the government gives its permission. Traditionally, governments have been slow to consent to suits, and the people in Washington have been no exception. Under the 1946 Tort Claims Act, the federal government has "waived" (agreed not to invoke) its immunity in some cases, but by no means all. For example, if a mail truck negligently driven by a Post Office employee runs into a car, the driver can sue, but if the Post Office negligently lost a letter costing a businessman a major contract, the businessman can only gnash his teeth, for the government will claim sovereign immunity.

An interesting tort suit was handled by a Court of Claims in 1960. Plaintiff was visiting her boyfriend in a Veterans Hospital; they began to argue and he shot her three times. Upon her discharge, she was presented a bill for $210 to cover the cost of hospitalization. She became furious, refused to pay, and sued the federal government for ten thousand dollars, claiming it was negligent by allowing one of its patients to sneak a gun into the hospital. She was awarded $2,500, minus the $210 hospital bill.

Cases that do not fall into any of these categories are argued in state courts. Most criminal cases fall into this category (except crimes committed in territory under federal jurisdiction, such as Washington, D.C.) and civil suits arising under state law. At times, however, the lines become hazy, and occasions arise when a lawyer must decide whether to bring suit in federal or in state court. A law, for instance, restricting freedom of press might seem to violate not only the federal Constitution but the state constitution as well. In these situations, legal strategy (attitudes of the respective judges, for example) may play as great a role as official rules in determining jurisdiction.

Federal Courts

Before we begin our journey through the maze of federal courts, we should discuss some features common to all of them. First, there is the manner of appointment. The Constitution gives the President the authority to appoint "judges of the Supreme Court" "with the advice and consent of the Senate" (i.e., approval in the Senate by majority vote). As for the other federal courts, the Constitution says, "he shall nominate, and by and with the advice and consent of the Senate, shall appoint . . . all other officers of the United States, whose appointments are not herein otherwise provided for, and which shall be established by law; but the Congress may by law vest the appointment of such inferior offices, as they think proper, in the President alone, in the courts of law, or in the heads of departments." In practice, Congress has not chosen to exercise any of those options regarding federal judges, and so they are all appointed by the President and confirmed by the Senate.

Judges hold office "during good behavior," which means that they stay on their court for life unless they are "impeached" and "convicted." Impeachment is a process of accusing, and requires that charges be brought by a majority of the House of Representatives. A trial is then conducted in the Senate, where a two-thirds vote is needed for conviction. According to the Constitution, the only grounds for conviction are "treason, bribery, or other high crimes and misdemeanors." The precise meaning of that list is unclear, but most scholars agree that conviction on a criminal charge is not necessary before impeachment may be voted. Since only thirteen people, including ten judges, have actually been impeached, and only four convicted, experience with the process does not fully repair the vagueness of the constitutional mandate. Judges, moreover, are immune to civil suits for damages caused while performing their duties; even if they act maliciously, their independence must be maintained.

As long as judges are in office, their salaries cannot be diminished; the purpose of this provision was to prevent anyone from punishing a judge for an unpopular decision. In 1920, the Supreme Court interpreted this guarantee to excuse judges from paying federal income tax, on the grounds that the tax reduced their income. This decision, made by judges for the benefit of judges, not surprisingly met with considerable resentment from the public at large, and in 1939 a different set of judges on the same Supreme Court took the unusual (though not unique) step of overruling their earlier decision, explaining that judges should pay taxes after all. More recently, in February 1976, fortyfour federal judges sued for a pay increase on the grounds that inflation had reduced the real value of their salaries, contrary to the constitutional guarantee. Twenty more judges joined the suit the next month, and a former Supreme Court justice, Arthur Goldberg, agreed to argue the case. Despite the distinguished clientele, their case does not appear to be very strong; but, then, we must remember that the ones they have to convince are not private citizens but other judges.

A final point all federal courts have in common is that their jurisdiction is restricted to cases and controversies. Before a federal court will hear a suit, it must be satisfied that real facts involving real opponents exist, and that these opponents have a legal interest that it is possible to determine and enforce. In short, the matter must be "justiciable." These requirements have given rise to a series of complicated rules, which even lawyers have difficulty understanding. The most complex of all is "standing," the rule that says that a party has the *right* to sue. Basically, a person must show that he is being injured in some legally recognizable way. Thus, if a person is hit in the face with pieces of a falling military aircraft, he or she would have standing to sue. The case of a taxpayer who believes that government is spending money improperly is less clear. Formerly, such persons had no standing and could do nothing, even if the government's actions were clearly unconstitutional. In 1968, however, the Supreme Court opened the door a bit to taxpayers' suits, at least in certain cases. Just how far open that door is has yet to be settled.

Connected with this question of justiciability is the rule against "friendly suits." A friendly suit is one in which both parties really want the same outcome. For instance, if a state government is offering a bond issue, a bank that wants to buy the bonds may first challenge the legality of the state's action just to be sure that the bank's investment will be safe. Both the state and the bank, of course, want the state to win the lawsuit. Because there is no real controversy, because both sides of the question will not be equally well represented, federal courts are supposed to dismiss such cases (although they do not always do so). The Supreme Court uses this same line of reasoning to reject pleas for "advisory opinions," in which people ask the court to make a ruling before doing something, so that they may know in advance if their actions will be legal. Indeed, even if there is a genuine controversy, if the issue involved seems to be too much of a "political question," better suited for the ballot box than the courts, the Supreme Court will refuse to decide it.

With all these rules, we must remember that it is the courts themselves that determine when they are to be applied and when not. The principles limiting standing may, therefore, be stretched when a court wishes to avoid getting involved in a particular dispute, or narrowed and restricted when a more activist court is concerned.

Supreme Court

The Constitution provides very little in the way of specifics regarding the Supreme Court. It establishes the "original jurisdiction" of the court, that is, the cases that may be heard first in the Supreme Court without being given prior consideration elsewhere: cases in which a state is a party, and those affecting ambassadors and other public ministers and consuls. Congress cannot enlarge this original jurisdiction, although it can give similar jurisdiction to other federal courts simultaneously. Beyond that, the guidelines are few. The Constitution does not set the number of justices for the court, nor does it impose a minimum age on its members; indeed, a justice need not be a lawyer, or even a U.S. citizen (although all justices have been both). All these matters are left to legislation.

Thus, Congress decides on the size of the Supreme Court, having fixed it at six in 1789. It was reduced to five in 1801, increased to seven members in 1807, nine in 1837, and ten in 1863, but was reduced again to seven in 1866 and changed back to nine in 1869, where it has remained. The primary reason for this increasing and decreasing size of the court was political, as for instance in 1801 (to prevent President Jefferson from filling a vacancy), and again in 1866 (so that President Johnson could not fill vacancies as they occurred). Increasing the court to nine members following Johnson's term permitted President Grant to appoint justices who would vote the right way in the *Legal Tender Cases*, in which paper currency issued by Congress was held to be legal money.

This kind of blatant political maneuvering has gone out of fashion, and is probably no longer possible. President Franklin Roosevelt certainly found this to be the case. When he assumed the presidency, FDR found a majority on the Supreme Court who did not share his views and demonstrated this by judicial decisions in conflict with New Deal philosophy, prompting him to propose a court-packing plan. The heart of the proposal was a provision that would have allowed the President to appoint one federal judge on the bench for those already serving who were over seventy. The size of the Supreme Court would then have increased to a maximum of fifteen. The idea aroused so much opposition, even among Roosevelt's supporters, that he had to withdraw it (on the other hand, the next year the court showed itself much less hostile to New Deal policies).

Nowadays, political manipulation of the court's membership is usually restricted to the appointment process, and this power is largely in the hands of the President. Although the Senate has rejected twenty-six of the 137 men nominated by Presidents for Supreme Court membership, only three of these rebuffs came in the twentieth century—one to Hoover and two to Nixon. A prudent chief executive, then, has a wide range of choice.

We are going to deal with an average in a moment, but before we do, it is well to recall the tragedy of the statistician who drowned in a pond that averaged only three feet in depth! On the average, American Presidents have made two appointments to the nation's highest tribunal during their tenure in office. Three (W. H. Harrison, who served only one month, A. Johnson, and Zachary Taylor) did not appoint any; Washington and FDR appointed eight each (not included in FDR's total is his elevation of Justice Stone to the chief justiceship in 1941). Seven appointed only one each, but then there were such Presidents as Taft (5), Jackson (5), Eisenhower (4), and Nixon (4), who helped raise the average.

Probably the first consideration a President takes into account in selecting a justice is the candidate's general philosophy. Judicial opinions reflect a number of things, including precedents and principles of law, but they also show the impact of the writer's social and economic views, and Presidents make an effort to choose justices with perspectives similar to their own. This is not to suggest that a President will be successful in every instance and choose individuals who will decide cases in such a way as to favor the President's views. The chances are that the *basic* similarities in philosophy between the two people will continue, with occasional differences, but a major breach can and does occur. For example, President Wilson, a liberal-minded President, appointed James McReynolds to the court, who became one of the most conservative (and cantankerous) justices—a "fixed-rock of enduring location." O. W. Holmes, Jr., became a bitter disappointment to Theodore Roosevelt. Prior to appointing him, Roosevelt had written Senator Lodge, "I should like to know that Judge Holmes [he was on Massachusetts' Supreme Judicial Court] was in entire sympathy with our views . . . before I would feel justified in appointing him." TR felt that Holmes betrayed him when Holmes's decisions reflected a view toward the function of the judiciary different from those of TR. More recently, three justices appointed by President Nixon joined in a unanimous opinion (with a fourth Nixon appointee not participating) compelling him to turn over to the special prosecutor's office tape recordings of his conversations, thus denying his claim of executive privilege.

Purely political factors have also played a role in appointments. Earl Warren became Chief Justice of the United States not because he was the greatest jurist in the land but as a reward for his support of Eisenhower in the 1952 Republican nominating convention and election. Byron White's appointment to the court resulted partly from the support he had given John Kennedy in the 1960 election, although a geographic factor was also involved. To make the court seem representative, Presidents like to have justices coming from all parts of the country, and White of Colorado took office as the only justice originating between Ohio and California. For many years, there was always one seat on the court occupied by a Jew, and there will undoubtedly be pressure to appoint another black to replace Justice Thurgood Marshall when he leaves the court. Party affiliation is a significant factor in appointments also; Democratic Presidents do not always pick Democratic justices, and Republican Presidents Republicans, but the exceptions are rare. Even personal friendship may weigh in a presidential decision, as it often did with Truman.

The question of the importance of a nominee's having previous experience as a judge is more controversial. Some Presidents have placed great emphasis on this item. For instance, Eisenhower considered such experience important, and four of his five appointees had served as judges in various federal or state courts. FDR, on the other hand, appointed eight people to the court and designated one Chief Justice during his twelve years and thirty-nine days in office, only two of whom (Murphy and Rutledge) had prior significant judicial experience. In general, prior judicial experience is not a high-priority item, and it is probably not as significant as other factors. The late Justice Felix Frankfurter (who had no judicial experience before joining the court in 1939), after reviewing the historical record, concluded: "One is entitled to say without qualification that the correlation between prior judicial experience and fitness for the Supreme Court is zero." The peculiar nature of Supreme Court business makes work on other types of courts relatively useless as training or preparation.

When a vacancy on the court occurs, members of Congress, interest groups, party leaders from all over the country, and other interested persons immediately come forth with recommendations for a successor. The Attorney General, with help from the FBI (for character checks), usually culls from these suggestions a list of possible candidates for the President's review. Often, the American Bar

Association (see Chapter 4) will be given a copy of the list and asked to classify the nominees as "qualified" or "not qualified"; the association has so far failed in its efforts to enlarge and formalize its role in the selection process. Even members of the court have been known to try to influence an appointment. When Justice Holmes retired, in 1932, his colleague Justice Harlan Stone urged President Hoover to replace Holmes with Chief Judge Benjamin Cardozo of the New York Court of Appeals, on the grounds that only a person of Cardozo's eminence could satisfactorily fill Holmes's seat (Cardozo was in fact chosen). There have been comparable cases.

We have already seen that the Constitution fixes the original jurisdiction of the Supreme Court. In reality, few cases reach the court under this rubric. Most cases the court deals with fall in its "appellate jurisdiction"; that is, the cases have been decided in lower tribunals and the losing party has asked the court to change the verdict. This appellate jurisdiction is determined by Congress, and the court itself has held that, absent express Congressional authorization, the court cannot hear an appeal.

Actually Congress has given the court considerable latitude in determining which cases it will review. The Judicial Act of 1925, which was drafted mainly by Chief Justice Taft and Justice Van Devanter and is known as the "Judges' Bill," provides the basis for the court's authority to select the cases it will hear. Only in two situations has Congress required that the court review a lower-court decision: where a state court has upheld the validity of a state law that has been challenged on the grounds of a conflict with the Constitution, a federal law, or a treaty, and where a state court has invalidated a federal law or treaty.

The most frequently used procedure for seeking a review by the Supreme Court is requesting that it grant a "writ of certiorari," which is, in effect, an order from a higher court to a lower court to hand up the records of the case for review. It does not mean the court will actually hear arguments on the case or even say more than "deci-sion of the lower court is affirmed." The person who says, "I'll take this case all the way to the Supreme Court" is probably a poor judge of distance; of the approximately ten million cases tried annually in state and federal courts, only about five thousand (1976) make it to the Supreme Court, nearly all on appeal. (Individual justices handled over twelve hundred applications, e.g. requests for "stays" —postponements of judicial action—during the same time period.)

Whether the court will grant certiorari or not is, really, up to the court under the very strict procedures and proper form contained in the court's Revised Rules. If four justices believe the issues raised in a request for re-view are of public importance and therefore appropriate for review by the full court, the writ is granted. Many times, these requests for review are coupled with written arguments from opponents indicating why the court should not grant the writ.

Clearly, this process of selection is a most important process in our system of government, because the granting of a review may have a significant impact on the political, social, and economic structures of the nation. There is, therefore, considerable interest in just what cases the court will accept. Generally, the court attempts to identify and accept those cases that will represent issues on which the court wishes to rule. Being in the right place, at the right time, with the right facts and situations can be very significant with regard to a decision by the Supreme Court.

A classic example of being in the right place at the right time was the 1961 case of *Mapp* v. *Ohio*. Mrs. Mapp, who had been arrested when police officers had found pornographic literature in her house, had appealed to the Supreme Court on the grounds of freedom of speech. The court took her case but ignored the free-speech question entirely. Instead, to the surprise of everyone (including Mrs. Mapp's attorneys), the court took the occasion to rule that the evidence seized by the police was not admissible in court since the police raid had been unconstitutional. Since Mrs. Mapp went free, one supposes she did not mind too much this unexpected line of reasoning, but the prosecution, and some dissenting justices, were quite perturbed. Many people had expected this ruling to come eventually, but no one had predicted it would come in this particular case.

Procedurally, requests for certiorari are filed with the Supreme Court's clerk along with any required or supporting materials; opposition arguments may also be filed within thirty days. At the end of the thirty days, each justice is given a copy of the papers, and anyone can place the request on the agenda for discussion. Four justices must agree before the case will actually be heard by the court.

There are two other ways to get a case to the Supreme Court. One, very rare, is by "writ of certification." A writ of certification is a request not from a private individual but from a federal court (usually one of the Courts of Appeals), for instructions on questions of law. More common, though rarely granted, is a type of certiorari submitted *"in forma pauperis."* This device affords an opportunity for people without funds or attorneys (e.g., prisoners) to gain access to the court without the use of attorneys. Instead, they write (often by hand) statements explaining their situation and the issue they wish to raise. These petitions are read and summarized by assistants to the Chief Justice, who distribute the summaries among the justices for their consideration.

The decision of which cases will be heard by the court is made during the court's conference, held Wednesday afternoons and all day Friday, and attended only by the justices. After all members have shaken hands (a custom dating back to 1888), they proceed to argue among themselves about the disposition of the approximately five thousand cases that face them each year. Normally, the Chief Justice presents the case, summarizes it, and puts forth his view on how it should be treated. The other justices proceed to give their opinions, with the most senior justice speaking first. Votes are taken in the same order.

Although the court has a variety of options in dealing with cases, the largest group—about 70 per cent—are simply dismissed without action. Some of the others will be referred back to lower courts for rehearing. Often, the court will deal with a case by means of a *"per curiam"* opinion: a brief, unsigned statement of the nature of the case and the court's decision. About two hundred of the cases will be scheduled for oral argument.

Usually, the court hears arguments for two weeks, then adjourns for two weeks to work on its agenda and its decisions. It meets from October to June in a Corinthian-columned building, just east of the Capitol, containing offices for justices, a cafeteria, lounges, a library, and of course, the courtroom itself. Seen from the small audience (there are seats for only about 180 people), there are tables for the lawyers, a lectern with small lights to warn the attorneys when their time is running out, and the raised table of marble and mahogany behind which sit the justices. To emphasize his independence, each justice may choose his own personal chair; the result is a motley collection of sizes, styles, and colors, backed by a line of red draperies. The Chief Justice sits at the center, the most senior associate justice on his right, the next most senior on his left, and so on.

The court's marshal opens the sessions by announcing, "Oyez, oyez, oyez [a term from English tradition meaning "hear ye"]. All persons having business before the Honorable, the Supreme Court of the United States, are admonished to draw near and give their attention, for the Court is now sitting. God save the United States and this Honorable Court!" (Some critics have rephrased that last sentence to read "God save the United States *from* this

Honorable Court.") After some minor business is disposed of, the court gets down to the business of hearing cases. The attorney for the party bringing the suit (or trying to get a lower court's decision changed) speaks first, followed by the attorney for the other side, and then rebuttal, if either attorney has saved some of his allotted time. The court typically gives no more than one half hour, or at most an hour, for each side, since most of the arguments have already been presented in written documents called "briefs." These briefs summarize the facts of the case as each side sees them, the issues in dispute, and the arguments each attorney plans to make; in addition, each side can respond to the other's brief. In the oral argument, the attorneys merely clarify and expand upon ideas expressed in their briefs, and try to persuade the justices of the merits of the case. Some justices will ask questions of counsel during the argument, either for information or to make some point of their own; other justices work at other matters; a few have been known to nap on the bench. Once the argument is completed, the attorneys leave (taking with them some quill pens as mementos), and the next case begins.

During the two-week intersessions, the justices review the arguments and briefs with the help of their "law clerks," recent law-school graduates who work for a justice as researchers and aides. They write and circulate draft "opinions"—statements of how they wish to decide the case and why. Justices read each other's opinions, accept them or make suggestions for changes, and eventually reach a final decision. This decision is then published, along with the opinion justifying it, as the "opinion of the court" or "majority opinion." A justice who agrees with the result but not the reasoning behind it may write a "concurring opinion"; a justice who rejects the decision itself may write a "dissenting opinion." Given the individuality of the justices, unanimous decisions are uncommon;

some difficult or controversial cases have drawn forth several opinions. For instance, when President Truman nationalized steel mills during the Korean War, it took the court nine separate opinions to hold his action unconstitutional (the vote was 6–3). Even worse, a justice may accept part of another justice's opinion but concur in or dissent from a different part of it. Interpreting Supreme Court decisions is thus a full-time job.

Of all the cases the court deals with, the most important are those dealing with whether state or federal government actions violate the U. S. Constitution. The court's power to declare a law unconstitutional is known as "judicial review" and dates back to a case in 1803 called *Marbury* v. *Madison* (although its roots go earlier). The facts of the case, which involved an effort by Marbury, a member of the Federalist Party, to get a government appointment granted him by Federalist President Adams but held up by Democratic President Jefferson and Madison, his Secretary of State, are of no real importance. What is significant is that the court and its Chief Justice, John Marshall, maintained that it had the right to find a legislative action to be in violation of the Constitution and therefore void despite the fact that no such power is mentioned in the Constitution itself. In practice, the court has usually been circumspect in using this power and has developed a set of rules to enable it to avoid constitutional issues whenever possible. Nevertheless, the court has invalidated about a hundred federal laws and a thousand state ones over the years, involving such issues as slavery, income tax, child-labor laws, racial segregation, prayers in public schools, birth control and abortion, and criminal procedure. These include the most controversial and momentous problems either the court or the country have ever met. The Supreme Court's ability to deal with such matters fairly and competently is a measure of its quality and of the future of the United States.

The Federal Court System

Congress derives its power to create courts from two separate provisions of the Constitution: Article I, which says, "Congress shall have power . . . To constitute tribunals inferior to the supreme court," and Article III, which says, "The Judicial power of the United States, shall be vested in one Supreme Court, and in such inferior courts as the Congress may from time to time ordain and establish." Consequently, Congress distinguishes between "legislative courts," established under Article I, and "constitutional courts," set up under Article III. The major difference between the two groups is that judges on legislative courts are not protected by the limitations placed by the Constitution on constitutional courts. Thus, judges on legislative courts may serve only for a specified period of time (instead of "during good behavior"), their salaries can be reduced, and their jurisdiction is not restricted by the rules of standing and controversy that apply in other courts. Whether a court is legislative or constitutional is determined solely by Congress, and there seems to be nothing to prevent Congress from changing the classification. At the moment, there are only two legislative courts: the Court of Military Appeals (for cases involving the military code) and the Territorial Courts (for possessions of the United States that have not received statehood). Constitutional courts dominate the federal judiciary.

Let us begin by looking at our chart and examining the organization and functions of these courts "inferior to the Supreme Court."

Just below the Supreme Court are the Courts of Appeals. Created by Congress in 1891 under the name "Circuit Courts of Appeals" (the name was changed in the Revised Judicial Code of 1948), the Courts of Appeals are "appellate" courts only, that is, they hear cases that have already been decided by another court when one of the

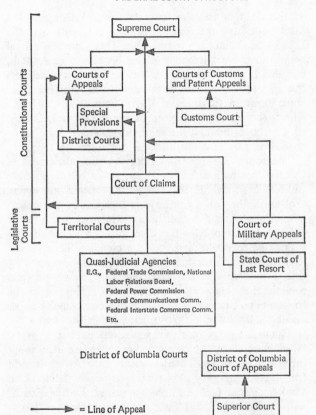

FEDERAL COURT STRUCTURE

District of Columbia Courts

⟶ = Line of Appeal

parties claims a mistake was made. In practice, appealing a decision is not so simple, since the mistake has to be of the proper type (as set down by Congress) or the case will be dismissed. These courts do dispose of many cases, though, and their workload has been increasing, from 2,830 trial cases in 1950 to 11,662 in 1970.

All together, there are eleven Courts of Appeals. Ten

of them are in the ten "circuits" (areas) Congress has
fixed throughout the country, while the eleventh is in the
District of Columbia (Washington, D.C., also has a local
court called the District of Columbia Court of Appeals,
but this is not a true national court). Congress also sets
the size of each court, with membership varying from
three to fifteen. At the head of each court is a chief judge,
who is the most senior person on the court below the age
of seventy. At seventy, the chief judge resumes his place as
an ordinary judge, although he is not forced to retire.

The courts usually divide themselves up into groups of
three judges to hear cases, which means the larger ones
can handle several hearings at once. For special and important cases, the entire court meets together, or "*en banc.*"
The judges also gather together at least twice a year in the
Judicial Conference for the Circuit, when they work "to
make all necessary orders for [the circuit's] effective and
expeditious administration." The chief judge also annually
calls a meeting of all federal judges in the circuit (and
sometimes all lawyers) to discuss affairs. The rest of the
time, a circuit executive chosen by the conference handles
all non-judicial administrative activities in the circuit.

The next level of courts are sometimes referred to as the
"work-horse courts." Not that other federal courts are not
busy, but the federal District Courts have a work load of
truly staggering proportions—over 325,000 matters each
year! Each state contains from one to four District Courts,
with each court having from one to twenty-seven judges
(the exact number is determined by Congress). There are
eighty-nine District Courts in the states and one for the
District of Columbia, adding up to some four hundred
judges. In addition, the territories of Puerto Rico, Guam,
the Virgin Islands, and the Canal Zone are also provided
with District Courts. As with the Courts of Appeals, the
senior District Court judge under seventy within the district is the chief judge. Each District Court has a professional administrator, clerk, marshal, U.S. district attorney

and assistants, referees in bankruptcy, probation officers, court reporters and assistants, and one or more magistrates (formerly called commissioners). Except for the U.S. attorney and the marshals (appointed by the President) and the assistant U.S. attorneys (appointed by the Attorney General), these personnel are selected by the judges.

The jurisdiction of the federal District Courts is "original," which means that cases are argued there first, before any appeal to a higher court. Usually, each court hears cases that arise in its district; removal of a case to another district is called a "change of venue" and occurs only in special circumstances. At the discretion of the Chief Justice of the United States, a District Court judge may be moved about to another district. For instance, a Wisconsin judge with expertise in taxes may be assigned to Iowa if a complicated tax case arises there. Each case is typically handled by a single judge, in contrast to the three-judge system of the Courts of Appeals. However, when someone is challenging the constitutionality of a state or federal statute, a special three-judge court may be convened, including two District Court judges and one Court of Appeals judge. This larger court is intended to guarantee more careful consideration of the arguments, and allows an appeal directly to the Supreme Court, bypassing the Appeals Court.

District Courts, of course, have jurisdiction only in federal cases. As we have noted, though, the line between federal and state matters is often wavy, and a good knowledge of the federal rules of civil and of criminal procedure is essential. It is sometimes possible to move to a federal court if one has lost in a state court, but the technique is complicated and the courts discourage it. One cannot simply "make a federal case" out of something anytime one wishes.

A special note about U.S. magistrates. Magistrates assist District Court judges by conducting pretrial or "discovery" proceedings to clarify issues before they reach the District Court judge. Magistrate's Court also handles petty offense and misdemeanor cases, and admiralty and civil claims and other important matters. In the past, magistrates were paid on a fee system; that is, they received a fee for each task they performed. The Federal Magistrates Act of 1968, however, professionalized the operation, putting magistrates on salary and requiring them to be attorneys themselves. Although Magistrate's Court remains in many ways a staff office to the District Court rather than a separate judicial body, its significance should not be discounted. In minor cases, a magistrate may drop charges altogether, and many defendants have found themselves out on bail thanks to an understanding magistrate.

In addition to these two sets of courts, which form a hierarchy from District Court up to Supreme Court, are also several specialized courts. Oldest of these is the Court of Claims, created by Congress on February 25, 1855, to resolve claims against the federal government in those situations in which it had waived sovereign immunity. It consists of a chief judge, six associate judges, fifteen commissioners, and support staff. The commissioners serve as pretrial personnel, gathering testimony and evidence and putting together the case, which then goes to the court *en banc*. Generally, the court tries non-tort claims against the federal government, such as compensation for the taking of property by the government, back federal pay, refund of income and excise taxes, breach-of-contract suits, and the like. (Tort suits are heard in District Courts.)

The Customs Court was established on June 10, 1890, with nine members, a chief judge and eight associate judges. This is one of two federal courts in which Congress has mandated bipartisan membership—no more than five of the judges can come from any political party. This court has exclusive jurisdiction under the tariff laws, including suits contesting appraisals by customs officials of

the value of imported merchandise. Usually judges sit in
divisions of three, but they may sit *en banc,* and valuation
cases are usually heard by a single judge. New York City is
the home port of this court, but judges do travel to other
major ports to hear cases. Furthermore, they may be tem-
porarily assigned by the Chief Justice of the United States
to hear District Court cases.

The Court of Customs and Patent Appeals is an appellate court that came into being by an act of Congress
on August 5, 1909. The five judges sit *en banc* to hear
cases on appeal from decisions in Customs Court. They
also hear certain appeals from decisions of the Patent
Office, the U. S. Tariff Commission, and some findings of
the Secretary of Commerce.

In 1950 Congress established the United States Court
of Military Appeals, a legislative court, to serve as a "GI
Supreme Court." Like Customs Court, it is bipartisan,
with no more than two of the three judges (who must be
civilians) coming from the same political party. Each
judge has a fifteen-year term. Its jurisdiction is appellate
from military tribunals, and while it has discretion as to
what cases it will hear, Congress has mandated that it
must grant appeal when a member of the military has
been court-martialed and sentenced to death or where a
flag officer (general or admiral) has been convicted by
court-martial. The decisions of the Court of Military Appeals are almost final, but the Supreme Court will take an
appeal if a fundamental constitutional right had been denied to the defendant.

The other legislative courts are those found in the territories. The jurisdiction of these courts is generally like that
of a District Court, except that they also have varying degrees of jurisdiction over local matters, depending upon
what it is Congress has authorized.

Oddest of all the federal courts is the Tax Court,
created in 1924. Unlike the other courts, the Tax Court is
not even part of the judicial branch of the government.

Instead, it is in the executive branch, with sixteen judges, appointed by the President and confirmed by the Senate, serving for twelve-year terms. Each judge, assisted by a court-appointed commissioner, travels around the country hearing cases from taxpayers involving such questions as tax deficiencies or overpayments in income, estate, and gift taxes. In effect, the Tax Court judges hear appeals from rulings of the Internal Revenue Service. Decisions of the court may be appealed to the appropriate Court of Appeals or the federal Court of Appeals in the District of Columbia, although with small sums the court's rulings may be final.

Finally, the District of Columbia has its own local court system. Since Washington, D.C., is not in any state, Congress has final authority for the laws and court system there. There are two important courts, the Superior Court and, above it, the District of Columbia Court of Appeals. Judges are appointed by the President for fifteen years, but they may be removed for cause by a special judicial commission.

Most of these courts work together in the Judicial Conference of the United States, founded by Congress in 1922. The conference, presided over by the Chief Justice of the United States, consists of the chief judges of the Courts of Appeals, one District judge from each circuit (elected every three years by the federal judges in the area), and the chief judges of the Court of Claims, the Customs Court, and the Customs and Patent Appeals Court. Once a year, the group assembles to discuss ways of improving the operation of the federal court system, to assign personnel for the coming year, and to advise Congress on laws regarding the judiciary.

Working closely with the conference is the Administrative Office of the United States Courts, established by Congress on August 7, 1939. This office is headed by a director appointed by the Supreme Court; a staff provides the necessary assistance to carry out its responsibilities of performing general administrative housekeeping assignments, preparing the budget for the federal court system (except the Supreme Court, which prepares its own), supervising federal probation officers and the Federal Public Defender Organization, and conducting studies of more effective ways to operate the federal judicial system. The office issues a report each year describing problems, studies, and recommendations regarding the federal judiciary. Further assistance to the federal judiciary is provided by the Federal Judicial Center, set up in 1967 "to further the development and adoption of improved judicial administration in the Courts of the United States." The center undertakes research and training programs designed to help those who have responsibilities within the federal judicial system.

One final problem of the federal courts is handled by the Judicial Panel on Multidistrict Litigation, established on April 29, 1968. Consisting of seven federal judges, it has the authority to transfer to a single District Court, for co-ordinated or consolidated pretrial proceedings, civil cases from various districts that involve common questions. This procedure adds to the efficiency of the entire system.

Judges

Like Supreme Court justices, all federal judges are appointed by the President. Political considerations enter into these selections even more than they do for the Supreme Court, and generally speaking, the lower-ranking the court the more significant are political factors. One item no President can ignore is the custom of "Senatorial courtesy," which gives senators of the same party as the President an unofficial veto power over judicial appointments in their states. Let us assume a federal District Court judgeship must be filled in a state. One or both senators from the state are of the same political party as the

President. Now, the President must consult with the senator(s) from the state over the appointment, because if he should nominate someone without such consultation and the senator(s) object in the Senate to the appointment, it is most unlikely the Senate will confirm, "as a matter of courtesy" to the senator(s) from the state. Why? The end result of this senatorial mutual-admiration arrangement is to give the senators a very strong voice in who gets the appointment; it provides them with just a little more patronage. The classic example of this system in operation occurred when Democratic President Truman attempted to fill six federal judgeships in Illinois without consulting with Illinois Senator Paul Douglas, also a Democrat. When the six nominees were presented by Truman, Douglas informed the Senate he objected to the appointments not because the nominees were not qualified but because the President had not discussed the names with him. The Senate refused to confirm. Truman submitted the same six names, Douglas once again objected, and the Senate did not confirm. Truman said the Constitution gave him the authority to appoint, not the Senate. Getting nowhere with this stand, he worked out a compromise with Douglas, yielding a list of six names—three from the old list and three new ones supplied by Douglas. The Senate confirmed when Douglas raised no objection.

Aside from senatorial courtesy, the Senate rarely refuses to confirm a judicial appointment. It will act, however, when a nominee is clearly not qualified. For instance, in the 1960s Lyndon Johnson appointed, at the request of the Kennedys, a Massachusetts politician for a judicial post. The nomination aroused so much furor, with opponents charging the individual with judicial incompetence, that the nomination had to be withdrawn (a more common procedure than actually voting a nomination down).

To help ensure judicial independence and the creation of an atmosphere in which judicial decision making can be made free of political pressures, nearly all judges have life tenure. They also have a reasonably decent salary structure (Court of Claims, $48,500; Customs Court and District Courts, $54,500; Customs and Patent Appeals, Military Court of Appeals, and Courts of Appeals, $57,500; Supreme Court, $72,000–$75,000 for Chief Justice—as of 1977), and enjoy a very liberal retirement plan. A federal judge may retire at full salary at seventy after ten years' service as a federal judge, or at sixty-five with fifteen years completed. This "inviting" retirement plan was also developed as an inducement for some of the more senior jurists—especially those on the Supreme Court—to retire and make room for another generation and, perhaps, more contemporary views.

Finally, while all federal judges are subject to impeachment (the only way to remove a life-tenured judge), this does not mean that an incompetent judge cannot be removed from hearing cases. For example, the Circuit's judicial council may remove a District Court judge from hearing cases, or it may call a judge before it to explain certain conduct. The Tenth Circuit's judicial council in 1966 relieved a District Court judge of his duties (they could not stop his salary from being paid, however) because of incompetency.

State Courts

Unlike the federal judiciary, there is no single state court system. Each state is free to arrange its courts as it wishes, and most states have at least one peculiarity not found in most other states. However, certain structures are typical of the majority of state court organizations, and we shall focus our attention on these.

Each state has a single court to serve as the ultimate court of appeals in state proceedings. The name varies, but "Supreme Court" is the most common, with New York using "Court of Appeals," "Supreme Court of Errors" in Connecticut, and "Supreme Court of Appeals" in Vir-

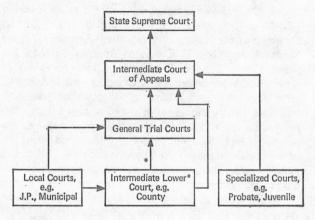

TYPICAL STATE COURT STRUCTURE

Line of Appeal

*Line of appeal depends upon case.

ginia. State constitutional and legislative provisions delineate the jurisdictional boundaries. Generally, these courts have appellate jurisdiction, with some original jurisdiction in certain cases. In some states, the highest court may (or even must) give the legislature or the governor advisory opinions concerning the constitutionality of proposed acts. The size of these courts varies, but it is usually an odd number, seven or nine judges being common. The judges are elected by popular vote in over half the states; the remaining states use gubernatorial appointment (e.g. Delaware), legislative appointment (e.g. South Carolina), or the "Missouri Plan," as found in Alaska, Nebraska, and eight other states, including, of course, Missouri. This plan utilizes a unique procedure which will be examined later. Terms of office vary, with ten years being typical.

About fifteen states, especially the most populous, have an intermediate appeal level between their general trial courts and the state's highest court of appeals. These courts are usually designated "Courts of Appeals," as in Missouri and California. The jurisdiction of these courts is typically appellate, and their jurisdiction is spelled out in state and/or constitutional provisions, based usually on the amount of controversy or the subject matter. The size of these courts varies, with terms ranging from four to fifteen years. Their selection is usually by election, but appointment by some process is also used. The primary function of this level of court is to provide some means of appellate action and to help reduce the work load on the state's highest court.

The third level consists of the general trial courts—"the work horses" of the state's judicial system. These courts of general jurisdiction handle civil, criminal, and equity matters (although a very few states, such as Delaware, maintain separate equity, or chancery, courts). Also, some states maintain separate courts for civil and for criminal cases. Thus South Carolina's Circuit Courts consist of two divisions: Common Pleas (civil) and General Sessions (criminal). In New York, a state general trial court (called, to the confusion of a lot of people, including New Yorkers, the "Supreme Court") handles mainly civil matters, while the county courts hear primarily criminal cases. Judges of these courts are usually selected by popular vote, either on a partisan or a nonpartisan basis. Some states provide for appointment by the governor (Rhode Island); the Missouri Plan is also used in a few states. Terms of office vary, from two years to life (good behavior, as in New Jersey and Massachusetts). Some states, e.g. New York, have a county court, which may have concurrent jurisdiction with the general trial court, or be below it but above those courts identified as being "minor."

These "minor" courts generally have very limited jurisdiction, handling only relatively unimportant civil and criminal matters. Judges are usually selected by popular vote with terms from two to four years. Within the wide range of these local courts, the two most interesting are the justices of the peace (J.P.'s) and Small Claims Court. J.P.'s are largely a rural phenomenon. Although they deal only with minor judicial questions, such as traffic violations and petty offenses, their impact should not be underestimated. They have very real powers at their disposal (in some states, they can put people in jail for up to a year), and the difficulty and expense of appeal make the bulk of their decisions final for all practical purposes. Regrettably, in many communities J.P.'s do not have law degrees, leading them to be somewhat arbitrary in their handling of cases. This tendency toward capriciousness used to be enhanced by a salary system whereby justices of the peace were paid by keeping the fines they levied, a method that did not encourage the niceties of fair play and due process of law. While this device has been declared unconstitutional by the Supreme Court, some local communities have not yet discarded it.

About thirty states provide for Small Claims Courts to settle civil disputes over small amounts of money (usually under five hundred dollars). Sometimes referred to as the "people's courts," their purpose is to negotiate compromises and acceptable settlements between parties in an informal atmosphere. Technical rules of procedure and evidence are not strictly enforced. Rather, the parties tell the judge their stories, the judge questions and then either makes a ruling on the spot or considers the problem further. In some states, to preserve the non-legalistic tenor of the proceedings, parties are not permitted to bring lawyers with them.

A number of localities offer methods of settling disputes requiring even less legal formality. They have "arbitration" and "mediation" services. Often run by private agencies, these consist of individuals trained in conflict resolution who meet with the disputants to help settle their differences. The difference between arbitration and mediation is that, with arbitration, the parties have agreed to accept whatever decision the arbiter makes, while they agree only to consider the proposals of a mediator. Although reliance on both mediation and arbitration is normally voluntary (unlike courts), they are so much less expensive and time-consuming than the judicial process that they are gaining popularity.

Typically, states also have specialized courts concerned with specific matters of law. Most common are courts dealing with juveniles, probating of wills, and domestic relations, but the variety is wider. For instance, Chicago has a Smokers' Court, which hears cases of those charged with violating a city ordinance prohibiting smoking in certain public places. Details concerning the operations of these courts and the methods of selecting judges differ from court to court and are usually specified in state constitutional or legislative provisions.

The most common method of selecting state judges is by popular vote, often with party competition. While this method is preferred by politicians, who have a large say in who gets nominated, and has some support among the electorate, it is criticized by lawyers as unprofessional. The public, they argue, is not really qualified to judge the judges, to evaluate how well a court is performing or how well qualified a candidate actually is. Instead, attorneys favor nomination by the chief executive as in the federal system, but with a screening process by practicing lawyers. Only the people who argue in court, they maintain, have the knowledge to determine how well a judge is doing.

The state of Missouri developed a combination of nomination and appointment for its judiciary which has received much praise from experts. Under the Missouri Plan, if a judge on the state Supreme Court, a Court of Appeals, or certain general trial courts seeks re-election, a vote is held, the judge running on his record, not against an opponent. If the judge wins, there is no problem. However, when a judge loses or does not even seek re-election, a nonpartisan judicial commission is set up composed of the state's chief justice, three laymen appointed by the governor, and three lawyers selected by the attorneys of the state. This commission presents the governor with a list of three names, from which he chooses one to serve for at least one year. Then that judge goes before the people for election to a full term, just like any other judge whose term has expired. Other states have similar procedures.

On the average, the quality of judges in American state courts, especially in the lower levels, is distinctly below that of the Western European states. British judges, for example, are usually chosen for their success as lawyers, while in the United States judges tend to get their jobs through political success. In France, a potential judge must attend the National School for Jurists for twenty-eight months to learn the tools of the judicial trade. The lack of required training in this country has led to consequences ranging from ludicrous to tragic. For instance, one Los Angeles municipal judge had to be removed for misconduct not merely because she heard cases with her Chihuahua dog on her lap and a mechanical canary trilling from her chambers but because upon being stopped by a police officer for excessive use of her car horn, she called him a male chauvinist and threatened him with "a .45-caliber vasectomy." A commission in Louisiana recommended disciplinary action against a city judge accused of deciding cases by flipping a coin or polling the spectators (including some cub scouts). On a more serious level, Oklahoma discovered in 1965 that three of its Supreme Court justices, including the chief justice, had been involved in corrupt practices, with one of them having sold his vote for several years. The effect on the morale of both the judiciary and the citizenry of such disclosures can easily be imagined.

In part to deal with such affairs, some states have looked for new ways to discipline or remove judges. All the states except Delaware, Hawaii, Indiana, and Oregon have provisions for impeachment of judges, and many permit removal by the state legislature, the governor, or the voters ("recall" elections). All these methods, though, are cumbersome and seldom used. Instead, some states have given the power to remove judges to more flexible institutions. In Michigan, the state's highest court can remove lower-court judges if there is cause. New York has a Court on the Judiciary, made up of six judges, who hear charges against other judges and have the power to remove them. New York also has a State Commission on Judicial Conduct to receive complaints against judges from private citizens or commission staff members, although the commission must refer charges to the Court on the Judiciary if a judge is to be removed. In other states, comparable structures exist.

Judicial incompetence, combined with the ever-increasing demands made on the courts, have led many specialists to demand sweeping changes in the judicial system. As far back as 1906, Roscoe Pound (1870–1964), a leading scholar of American law, called for major reforms, including nonpartisan judges, streamlined court procedures, and better lawyers. Chief Justice Warren Burger has made this a special cause of his own; his suggestions entail fewer appeals and better practical training for attorneys. In the structural and organizational realm, the National Municipal League (devoted to improving local governments) has proposed a "unified court system." This system would eliminate the multiple court structures in each state in favor of a single organization which would consist of divisions and branches. The entire system would be controlled by a central administrative authority, perhaps the chief justice. Alaska, Michigan, and North Carolina have been moving toward such a system.

That so many distinguished people and groups have spent so much time devoting their attention to improvement of the courts indicates not only the weaknesses of current arrangements but also the significance they see resting in the judiciary. Were it not for the vital role courts play in our lives, fewer people would bother to criticize them or try to alter them. Overworked and underqualified as they may be, the nation's judges have a major impact on the lives of all Americans.

4
The Legal Fraternity

Most societies have specialists to apply the rules of the culture. It may be the tribal elders, whose memories of past disputes serve as the basis for resolving present ones. It may be priests, trained in the knowledge of the will of the deity. In some places, such as China, it has been scholars, masters of the written traditions. But almost always there is someone, some group to whom the people appeal when they are perplexed about what is right and proper.

In the United States, to a large extent this role is played by lawyers. To be sure, few of us look to attorneys for moral or spiritual guidance; the image of lawyers held by some places them somewhat below Attila the Hun in ethical qualities. A person who seeks to know the rules, however, who wishes to discover what can or cannot be legally done, turns immediately to a lawyer for advice. Businesses, labor unions, churches, athletes, all rely on legal counsel in their affairs.

The way lawyers are trained and the way they are organized, therefore, is a matter of considerable importance for everyone. For many, this point was brought home in the Watergate crisis. If most lawyers resemble those who planned, carried out, and justified the activities that forced Richard Nixon to resign, then we are all in trouble. On the other hand, if the lawyers who helped uncover and prosecute the perpetrators of the Watergate conspiracy are typical of the profession, America is in reasonably good hands. We turn, then, to an examination of lawyers in the United States today.

Legal Education

Until the mid-nineteenth century, the study of law in the United States entailed a combination of apprenticeship and the reading of such classic lawbooks as Blackstone's *Commentaries*. Formal courses in law were few. The breakthrough in legal education came at Harvard Law School under the leadership of Christopher Langdell (1826–96). Langdell believed the best way for students to learn the principles of law was to study the judicial opinions of appellate-court judges whose decisions embodied these principles. To achieve this goal, he introduced the "casebook," an edited collection of major opinions on a given topic. Students were expected to read these opinions before coming to class. In the classroom, the teacher would describe hypothetical situations requiring application of the principles from the cases, and students discussed how the hypothetical case should be resolved (in law schools, this is known as the "Socratic method").

The casebook method emphasizes analytical skills, reasoning ability, and clear expression of ideas. While no one questions the value of these abilities for a lawyer, many critics have argued that there are gaping inadequacies in the training of lawyers today. Some suggest a need for more relevant and up-to-date courses in the frontier areas of law: rights of the poor, law of the sea, environmental law, and so on. Others bemoan the lack of moral stature among young attorneys, and demand a more ethical approach to the study of law. As we have mentioned, prominent legal figures, including Chief Justice Warren Burger, have complained that lawyers have insufficient preparation to engage in genuine courtroom practice.

In 1973, this last problem led Chief Judge Irving Kaufman of the Second Circuit Court of Appeals to appoint a panel of twenty-three judges, lawyers, and educators, under the leadership of President of the American College of Trial Lawyers Robert Claire, to prepare suggestions on improving the quality of courtroom advocacy. The panel came in with recommendations requiring lawyers to pass courses in evidence, civil procedure, criminal law, professional responsibility, and trial advocacy. The federal judges within the Second Circuit voted down the proposals, but the Claire panel nevertheless reflected some widely shared concerns about legal training.

Some states have looked to postgraduate education as the best method for upgrading legal performance. In Iowa, for example, lawyers must complete fifteen hours of legal education a year even after they have left law school. Other states are experimenting with legal specialists. A lawyer could be certified as a specialist in a certain aspect of the law, but only after meeting certain standards above and beyond law school. From outside the profession, some consumer groups are looking for ways to rate lawyers, as well as calling for attorneys to advertise their fees. All of these complaints have had their effect on law schools, and so the casebook method is not as dominant as it was thirty years ago. Schools now provide "clinical education" (work in real-life settings), "moot court" (trial of hypothetical cases before experienced judges and attorneys), courses in professional responsibility, and other educational innovations. However, the critics, and even many law schools themselves, are far from satisfied with the results.

Deficient or not, law school remains almost the only way a person can enter the legal profession. Admission into law school has thus become a desirable commodity, and competition is fierce. Figures vary from year to year, but about three times as many people take some steps to go to law school as actually get in. Law schools have therefore had to develop methods and criteria to enable them to choose among their excessive number of applicants.

One screening device, deemed notorious by some critics, is the Law School Admission Test (LSAT). Developed for the law schools by the Educational Testing Service (ETS), a non-profit corporation in Princeton, New Jersey, the test purports to measure the abilities necessary for a successful first-year law student. The test is divided into two parts. The larger section tests powers of reasoning and comprehension; grades range from 200 to 800, with a mean of 522. The "Writing Ability" section focuses on the use of the English language, with scores ranging from 20 to 80 (mean, 50). Over the past few years, over one hundred thousand people annually have taken this test, and law schools have spent much effort determining how valid its predictions are. The current consensus seems to be that, taken in conjunction with undergraduate grades, the "law boards" are a fairly good, though not spectacularly accurate, measure of law-school potential, at least for the first year of school.

Hence, many law schools place weight on Undergraduate Grade Point Average (UGPA). As with the LSAT, the higher the grade the better the chances of admission. Law schools can take grade inflation into account by using a guidebook, prepared by ETS, that lists the overall school UGPA in all participating colleges. Taken together, the LSAT score and the UGPA are normally the two most important elements in any applicant's folder.

Law schools do not require any particular "pre-law" college curriculum or major. Of course, they do insist on substantive work: an "A" grade in a course titled "Art of Tapping Beer Kegs" will likely be dismissed. The content of the work, and the major field of study, however, are left to the discretion of the student. The one thing law schools do recommend is a broad liberal-arts background. In the words of the late U. S. Supreme Court Justice Felix Frankfurter:

No one can be a truly competent lawyer unless he is a culti-vated man. If I were you, I would forget all about my technical preparation for the law. The best way to prepare for the law is to come to the study of the law as a well-read person. Thus alone can one acquire the capacity to use the English language on paper and in speech and with the habits of clear thinking which only a truly liberal education can give. No less important for a lawyer is the cultivation of the imaginative faculties by reading poetry, seeing great paintings in the original or in easily available reproductions, and listening to great music. Stock your mind with the deposit of much good reading, and widen and deepen your feelings by experiencing vicariously as much as possi-ble the wonderful mysteries of the universe, and forget all about your future career.

Are law-school admission criteria based completely on quantifiable factors? No, although the LSAT and UGPA have developed into the two principal criteria for admis-sion. Letters of recommendation *may* be of some value if they really get to the heart of the matter and describe the candidate's intellectual ability, industriousness, quality of character, and other positive factors. It would also be of help, perhaps, if the person writing the letter were presi-dent of the law school's board of trustees! A nice, friendly letter from nearly everyone (including mayors, congress-men, judges, lawyers) informing the admissions committee of what a delightful and charming person the applicant is, will not in itself enhance the chances of admission.

If one can present evidence of goal setting and con-certed effort to realize such goals, of good moral character, maturity, of an ability to think clearly and logically, these would be positive factors worthy of consideration by an admission committee. Law school is very hard work. Law schools must search out qualities in people's total makeup that indicate they might be able to merit the rigors and

demands of studying law. Naturally, law schools are eager
to provide seats to those who, from all indications, will
begin and complete the study of law and be a credit to the
profession. One can appreciate the dilemma many admission people face when they must inform *qualified* applicants that it is not possible for them to be admitted simply because there is "no room at the inn."

Still more complex is the situation of applicants from
groups whose enrollment in law schools has traditionally
been low: women and racial and ethnic minorities. With
women, the problem has been a social prejudice against
women attorneys which has discouraged women from con-
sidering a legal career. Those who have braved the tradition have encountered professors who would not take female students seriously, and law firms whose first question
of any woman job applicant, no matter how prestigious
her law school, was always "Can you type and take dicta-
tion?" The modern feminist movement has had a substantial impact on these conditions. Indeed, there are now
some law schools that have a majority of women students,
and the general status of women in the legal profession,
while still far from perfect, has nevertheless improved considerably.

Racial and ethnic minorities present another problem.
Not only have they met with prejudice and discrimination,
but many of them charge that the normal criteria for admission to law school, especially the LSAT and the
UGPA, are culturally biased. They argue that, although
minority-group members are just as talented as whites, the
society has forced them to develop their abilities in ways
that the law boards and college grades do not adequately
measure; therefore, admissions for minority-group applicants should, in fairness, rely on more relevant characteristics.

This position, persuasive as it may be, naturally draws
objections from those individuals who are refused admission in favor of people with lower numerical records. This

is a tricky issue, and even the Supreme Court chose to evade it in the *DeFunis* case (a suit brought by white student Marco DeFunis, who had been denied admission at the University of Washington Law School, while minority candidates with lower scores were accepted). In the meantime, the legal status of "preferential admissions" remains in doubt, as does the future of the Council of Legal Education Opportunity (CLEO), "designed to serve those economically and educationally disadvantaged persons." CLEO was established in 1968 to provide special help to minority-group members to prepare them for law-school work, but its continued funding is now in question. Thus, while the number of lawyers from minority groups has increased in the past decade, the future is not assured.

Entering law school is not the same as becoming a lawyer. There are two requirements in most states for winning the right to practice law: a degree from an "accredited" law school, and a passing grade on the state "bar exam," a test covering the specific laws of the state. Law schools receive their accreditation either from the American Bar Association (to be discussed later in this chapter) or from the state in which the school is situated. In principle, accreditation certifies that the law school meets certain minimal requirements for adequate legal education, such as a trained faculty, good library, proper courses, and so on. The accreditation process has definitely raised the quality of legal training in the United States; unaccredited law schools should therefore be looked on with suspicion. Desperate law students, rejected at all the law schools they applied to, who enroll in the Benedict Arnold College of Law and Tractor Repair are usually wasting their time and money.

A better alternative for those with legal interests but no acceptances in law school is a career as a "paralegal." Paralegal-training programs teach an individual to work as a lawyer's assistant, helping in legal research, writing, tax preparation, etc. In practice, much of the work done by a lawyer does not actually require full legal training, so the demand for paralegals has been increasing. Again, there are dubious programs seeking to cash in on a new market, but careful investigation can enable one to select an institute that provides high-quality education.

The outlook for the legal profession is uncertain. On the one hand, some economic projections estimate an oversupply of lawyers by the 1980s. Others indicate an unfulfilled need for legal services for the poor and middle class, and predict an abundance of job opportunities for the next several years. Whatever happens, there will always be new problems and institutions in our society, which require new attorneys to handle them.

Practice of Law

Having received the law degree—an LL.B. (Bachelor of Laws) or a J.D. (Doctor of Jurisprudence, the LL.D. being an honorary degree) and passed the state bar exam, what does a lawyer do? The record in New York is probably typical: 11 per cent work for government, 77 per cent enter private practice, and 12 per cent take positions with private corporations or similar employment. Due to the increased complexity and variety of law, no single lawyer can grasp all its technicalities and special features. Consequently, lawyers have grouped in law firms, which permit specialization and save costs (on lawbooks, for example). Fewer than half of this nation's lawyers practice alone. Simplicity in life is hard to find and maintain in the vast urban industrial society of today.

Those attorneys who do practice solo deal with all kinds of laws and perform a variety of legal functions both in their offices and in courtrooms. Some can adequately and properly manage their tasks; others cannot, and the quality of legal service delivered may be low. Individual practice is difficult. For one thing, there are many skills to master. Becoming an effective trial lawyer, for example, requires much training and practice, which a single attorney cannot often afford. England and France, in fact, divide lawyers into those who handle courtroom trials (barrister or *avocat*) and those who do the paperwork (solicitor or *avoué*). Major law firms in the United States usually have trial specialists to deal with such matters. Obviously, an individual lawyer is at a disadvantage trying to be competent in this as well as other skills.

Moreover, there are factors that work to lower the reputation of individual practitioners. It is not unheard of for some attorneys to have "investigators" seek out cases to bring to court, even when no real claim exists. Such "ambulance chasing" is unethical, but substantiating charges of improper conduct is not easy. In addition, messy cases, such as nasty divorces, are often referred to solo lawyers by firms that want to avoid bad publicity. The lot of an individual attorney is thus not an easy one.

At the same time, solo practice can be very rewarding both financially and personally. The variety inherent in dealing with differing aspects of law provides a challenge and sense of satisfaction that specialization often lacks. Many solo lawyers prefer the one-to-one relationships they can develop with their clients to the more impersonal atmosphere of a large firm. Finally, it is often possible to use the training and contacts developed in individual practice to launch a political career; more politicians come from legal backgrounds than from any other source. While few people grow up to be President, it is not uncommon for a lawyer to open an office in a small town, build a clientele, serve on the town council for a period, and earn a position as an honored and respected member of the community. Surely, not an unattractive prospect.

It is also becoming standard practice for businesses to have what are termed "house counsels." That is, a company will hire an attorney or attorneys who will work for the company on a full-time basis, taking care of whatever legal work arises. Because of the numbers of business firms in the country and the amount of governmental and legal regulations directed at them, having a lawyer or two on the staff is not only convenient but almost necessary. Small companies usually have general counsels as their legal advisers, but larger firms will often have specialists for each type of problem they encounter.

Government has always contained lawyers within it, and the number has been growing steadily. As laws have grown in number, so, too, has the need for more lawyers to enforce them. Whether this government of the lawyers, by the lawyers, for the lawyers is a good idea or not is no longer really an issue, except for anarchists. We have a big government because we need and want one. How efficiently the government operates, and its impact in specific cases, are, of course, other questions, but ones we shall not seek to answer here.

Regardless of where they work, lawyers work in similar ways. For one thing, most of them spend more time writing and reading than anything else. The mental scene of the Perry Mason-type counselor skillfully and eloquently pleading a case at the bar that results in justice for all and not a dry eye in the courtroom, is one in which most American lawyers would never appear, by chance or by choice. Rather, attorneys will devote considerable time and energies to negotiating over matters on behalf of their clients in an effort to prepare a contract that will protect their interests, settling a dispute without the need of a court trial, arranging for a divorce that will preserve their clients' rights, or serving as a sounding board or just as an adviser on a number of non-legal matters.

When one is summoned to join the celestial choir, temporal matters require attention, and it is the lawyer who probably assisted in this area by drawing up the proper will, creating necessary trusts, looking out for tax advantages that would lessen the tax burden on the estate and individual inheritances, etc. Criminal charges, naturally, soon involve legal services. Failing to keep a client out of jail, the attorney will attempt to arrange for release from police custody and try to have the charges reduced or dismissed based upon procedural and substantive matters. If that fails, he will represent the individual at trial and, if necessary, pursue the avenue of appeal if a conviction takes place. Buying a house, an office building, a piece of land, or other property usually requires the assistance of counsel because of the need to investigate important legal points. For example, does the person selling you a house really own it: does he or she "have title"? Are there any restrictions in the deed that may preclude the buyer from using the property in a particular way? Is there, perhaps, some kind of easement that goes with the land (as in the North-South dispute in Chapter 2) that guarantees someone else the legal right to make use of the land in some way? All these questions, and others, should be determined by lawyers *before* the purchase is made, or they will be fought out in court afterward.

In addition to such personal services, lawyers are also becoming more active in "public-interest law." Public-interest law includes two distinct but related elements: representing clients who cannot afford to pay regular fees (the poor, certain charitable organizations, and the like), and serving the broad public good instead of special interests. Traditionally, attorneys have taken selected cases of these types on a *pro bono publico* basis, i.e. as a matter of public service and without charge. The past two decades, though, have seen the rise of organizations solely dedicated to this kind of legal practice. For instance, the Center for Law in the Public Interest, a non-profit firm in Los Angeles, has undertaken several major lawsuits, including cases involving illegal corporate campaign contributions in the 1972 election. Other groups, such as Common Cause and Ralph Nader's Public Citizen, although not engaged exclusively in legal action, still retain lawyers and handle significant cases (such groups are aided by the fact that,

unlike legislative lobbying, bringing court suits does not violate the rules for tax-exempt status).

In 1975, grants from a few charitable foundations were
assigned to the Council for Public Interest Law to clarify
and expand the functions of public-interest law. The council, chaired by former United States Attorney General
William Ruckelshaus and former Assistant Attorney General Mitchell Rogovin, has thirteen members, both practicing lawyers and law-school professors. The council is studying methods of financing public-interest law through
federal grants, prepaid-legal-service programs, and the creation of public-interest counsels within state governments.
As the field expands, so, too, will the number of lawyers
engaged in it.

Financing public-interest law is itself only one part of
the larger problem of financing legal costs in general. Attorneys' fees, like the cost of so many things, are going up.
In some of the larger and more prestigious firms, hourly
rates may range from thirty to sixty dollars an hour
just for an associate member, and up to one hundred fifty
dollars an hour for a genuine partner. In one "class action"
suit (a group of people with the same grievance joining together to bring a case—see Chapter 6), a law firm received
over four million dollars for its six years of work. It is not
surprising that the gross earnings of lawyers rose from two
billion dollars in 1955 to almost ten billion in 1972, and
have continued to rise.

Some people, no doubt, are wealthy enough to afford to
pay a lawyer sixty to one hundred dollars an hour. At the
poverty level, people may receive counsel through *pro
bono publico* services, through Legal Assistance Corporations (funded by federal and local governments), Legal
Aid Societies, or public-defender programs. The middle
class, however, may easily be caught literally in the
middle.

The fixing of legal fees thus becomes a major consideration in the practice of law. For certain functions,

charges are based on the service performed. For example, the fee for probating a will may be assessed on a sliding scale: 7 per cent on the first seven thousand dollars, 5 per cent on the next four thousand dollars, and so on. Arrangements of this sort are common—so common, indeed, that they have been challenged as violating anti-trust laws. In personal-injury suits, an attorney often works on a "contingency fee"; that is, if the client wins, the attorney gets one third to one half of the money, while if the client loses, the attorney gets nothing. The possibilities for abuse of this system by unscrupulous lawyers, either by cheating their clients or by manufacturing "nuisance" suits to win settlements, are obvious, but without this device it is hard to see how many people could afford to have their rights vindicated in court.

Another means devised to help offset the cost of legal assistance is "prepaid legal insurance." Under this system, an organization pays money each year to a panel of lawyers in exchange for a certain number of hours of legal advice. Labor unions in particular have begun investigating prepaid legal insurance as a benefit for members comparable to health insurance. Some states are going further and exploring a plan to allow individuals as well as groups to obtain legal insurance. Until such insurance becomes widespread, or some other way is found to pay legal costs, people will continue to be denied full access to the skills and talents of the legal fraternity.

The Bar

As we said, not everyone who finishes law school becomes a practicing lawyer. Legal training is also useful for individuals seeking careers in business, in accountancy, in police work, or in teaching, none of which require one to practice law. If one has been licensed as an actual lawyer, one is said to be a "member of the bar" (the bar refers to the separation between the audience and the judge in a courtroom).

As mentioned above, most states require a would-be attorney to complete law school and pass a bar exam. However, each state makes its own rules, and there are variations. Louisiana, for example, does not require a bachelor's degree to be accepted at the bar; three years of college and three of law school suffice. Most states do require a college degree. In a few states, it is possible to practice law without completing law school if one has served an apprenticeship in a law office (this path is rarely taken even where it is available, since regulations on apprenticeships are strict, and few law firms can afford the time and effort to meet them). The format of the state bar exam also varies from state to state, as, of course, does its content.

As a general rule, a person licensed to practice in a state may also appear before the federal courts in that state. To argue before the Supreme Court, one must have practiced for five years and be recommended by two attorneys already admitted to the Supreme Court bar. Moving from one state to another raises other problems. Normally, a lawyer accepted in one state can work in another for a particular case, although it is customary for a local attorney, the "counsel of record," to be present. Some states have reciprocity agreements whereby any lawyer licensed in one state can also be admitted to the bar of the second. Otherwise, the attorney must take the bar exam in the new state just like any law-school graduate.

Lawyers are often members of bar associations. Bar associations were first organized in the 1870s as part of an attack on official corruption. Membership was voluntary, usually consisting of lawyers seeking influence in the judicial system. In 1913, lawyers formed the American Judicature Society to improve the quality of legal practice. Its primary goal was the establishment of an "integrated bar," requiring any attorney wishing to practice law in a state to become a member of its bar association (i.e., a closed shop). About thirty states have integrated bars; some have been ordained by state legislatures, others by the state's highest court.

There are approximately seventeen hundred bar associations in the United States, ranging from small, local groups to special-interest associations: the American Trial Lawyers Association, the Maritime Law Association, the National Bar Association (made up of black attorneys), and so on. Dominating them all, however, is the two-hundred-thousand-strong American Bar Association (ABA).

The ABA operates through a system of committees and subcommittees, called sections, that are made up of lawyers who have a particular interest in some area of the law, e.g. criminal or anti-trust law. The ABA has become the national co-ordinating body for the nation's bar associations because its membership is not limited to just individuals; since 1936, state and local bar associations have become members. It is today a very influential body which works for legislation, rules, and policies that it believes to be in the best interest of the legal profession. Its influences on what will be required in the way of bar examinations have, of course, a pronounced effect on what is taught in law schools. The selection of federal judges is also an area in which the ABA has played an increasing role.

While the necessary professional regulations and appropriate disciplinary measures are officially produced in the state, they usually follow the guidelines laid down first in the "Canons of Professional Ethics" developed by the American Bar Association in 1908, and later in a statement of standards called the "Code of Professional Responsibility." The code has three parts: canons, disciplinary rules, and ethical considerations. A recent change in the code, adopted by the ABA's 340-member House of Delegates at its 1976 meeting in Philadelphia, will give an indication of the types of issues it covers and of its relation to state rules. The new clause permits attorneys to advertise in the yellow pages of telephone books, indicating office hours, field(s) of concentration, names of regular clients, and what credit cards, if any, are acceptable. It would also be possible for the attorney to indicate the initial consultation fee, and, upon written request, a schedule of fees and an estimate for services. These changes, brought about by extensive pressures from internal and external sources on the ABA, do not mean that lawyers may now rush out and purchase space in the yellow pages. State bars must adopt the changes or portions of them before such activity is within the professionally acceptable practices of the states. Assuming non-acceptance by state bar associations, advertising by attorneys within such states would constitute a violation of the states' professional requirements and subject the violators to disciplinary action by the state bar association. In practice, however, many states, perhaps most, will follow the ABA's lead and change their rules.

The code also forms the basis for rules on professionally acceptable conduct, although, again, there are state variations. Typically, complaints against an attorney are filed with the appropriate bar association or with a court (usually an appellate court). The bar association investigates the charge, holding formal hearings in the case of major complaints, and either persuades the parties to settle their differences or makes a recommendation to the designated disciplinary body (usually the state's highest court). The recommendation can call for dismissal of the accusation, reprimand, suspension, or disbarment.

A reprimand is a formal notation that a lawyer's professional conduct has been unacceptable and that a warning to this effect has been made by the appropriate judicial body. In itself, its effects are moral and psychological rather than material, but a second violation may result in a more severe penalty.

The severe penalties are suspension and disbarment.

During a period of suspension, an attorney is forbidden to practice law within the state where the penalty has been imposed. Disbarment is permanent suspension. If a lawyer is disbarred, he is prohibited from practicing law forever. Since it effectively denies a person the right to earn his livelihood in the way he was trained to do, disbarment is restricted to the most flagrant cases of professional wrongdoing (about 150 per year nationwide).

Bar associations support and co-operate in such disciplinary arrangements partly to uphold the standards of their profession and partly for fear that if they do not regulate themselves, outsiders will do it for them. Despite these exhibitions of professional responsibility, the bar, and especially the ABA, have not escaped severe criticism. Bar associations have been accused of being more concerned to preserve the privileges and incomes of their members than to secure the public good. Consumer groups have charged the bar associations with price fixing and other monopolistic practices, while civil libertarians have accused them of racial, religious, and sexual discrimination. Finally, the spectacle of twelve practicing attorneys being indicted or convicted in the Watergate affair has not added luster to the profession.

The ABA and the other bar associations have responded to much of this criticism. The change in the code to allow advertising, and the ABA's recent approval of prepaid legal insurance (aspects of which it opposed until 1975), have been gestures in the direction of consumer activists. Similarly, its cosponsorship of CLEO in 1968 aimed at improving its record on minorities. These and other activities by the ABA have gone part of the way in correcting those weaknesses fastened on by its critics.

The Reputation of the Legal Fraternity

Despite their virtues, bar associations, and lawyers in general, face a major obstacle in their efforts to enhance the image of their profession: lawyers are simply not popular in American society. Typical are the comments of W. Allen Wallis, chancellor of the University of Rochester, in his address to a recent graduating class of the university's medical school: "Lawyers have you outnumbered . . . but on the average they are no match for you in intelligence or dedication. Just don't let them ambush you while you are absorbed in caring for the sick." Mr. Wallis was especially disturbed by malpractice suits (or, at least, by successful malpractice suits); and, of course, the University of Rochester has no law school. Nevertheless, many people would undoubtedly endorse his views about lawyers (though perhaps not about doctors), and some might even join with the character in Shakespeare's *Henry VI, Part 2*: "The first thing we do, let's kill all the lawyers." Certainly, no vision of Utopia ever includes a bar association.

Part of the reason for this low reputation, aside from the instances in which it is obviously deserved, relates to the peculiar ethics of the legal profession. Most people, for example, consider it immoral for a lawyer to defend a client the lawyer believes is guilty. Yet, most attorneys consider it immoral to refuse a case on such grounds. At issue is not, as cynics might suppose, the size of the fee. Lawyers argue that our system has placed the decision of guilt or innocence in the hands of judge and jury, not attorney. For lawyers to make the decision on their own would be to short-circuit the judicial process and to deprive defendants of the rights guaranteed them by the Constitution. The system works because each element involved does its job; the lawyer's job is, essentially, to defend.

More troublesome questions arise in civil disputes. For instance, if a landlord asks a lawyer to prepare a lease that is legally acceptable but, in the lawyer's opinion, unfair, what should the lawyer do? Most would do the job, although many would point out to the landlord the questionable aspects of the document. The argument here is that lawyers are not trained moralists. What might appear to an attorney as unfair might in fact be accepted as just by, let us say, a minister or ethical philosopher who is professionally trained to deal with moral issues. When lawyers pass moral judgments on their clients, they are moving unjustifiably beyond the boundaries of their expertise.

Positions such as these, however sincerely advocated, look suspiciously self-serving to an outside observer. Charges of hypocrisy, though not entirely fair, are not entirely beside the point either. Lawyers are caught in difficult ethical situations, and like most people, they find it easier to decide hard cases in their own favor. This does not mean that they are wrong, but it does not enhance their popularity.

A second basis for our dissatisfaction with the legal fraternity is the demands we make on them. We have already noted the variety of issues law deals with in our society, and the list is constantly expanding. In the United States, every grievance becomes a lawsuit, every dispute a legal question. Our basic trust in law is no doubt commendable. When taken to extremes, however, it leads us to place demands on the law and its practitioners that they simply cannot humanly be expected to meet.

We should not expect too much from our legal institutions. Much they can do, and some of it they do well. Much remains, though, that citizens must do for themselves. Just as big government can become obstructive of its own ends, so, too, can law. As the Dutch philosopher Baruch Spinoza (1632–77) said, "He who tries to fix and determine everything by law will inflame rather than correct the vices of the world." Ultimately, for all the importance of law, people must deal directly with each other if our problems are to be solved.

5

Homemade Law

One of the first things most Americans learn about government is that there are three branches, each doing its own special job: the legislative branch makes the laws, the executive enforces them, the judicial interprets them. The second thing they learn is that this division is oversimplified to the point of inaccuracy.

Of course legislatures make laws. But they have no monopoly of that power. Courts, too, make laws, and not only the Supreme Court but lower-level judges as well. Then there are administrative agencies, sometimes part of the executive branch, sometimes independent, which have lawmaking powers of their own. Finally, our society has placed broad power to regulate conduct in the hands of private citizens directly, without their having to wait for any government body to act. The agreements they make are called contracts.

Contracts

Contracts are privately created laws fixing the rights and responsibilities of the parties making the contracts. Used in a wide variety of contexts, from business to marriages, contracts combine two basic advantages: they provide the flexibility necessary to deal with the innumerable different relationships that arise in society, and they provide assurance that one person or corporation can rely upon the promises of another. This combination of flexibility and assurance permits people to engage in transactions that would otherwise be impossible.

A contract can be entered into by an individual, a corporation, or a governmental body. However, legally binding contracts that courts will enforce (and there is not much point making any other kind of contract) can be made only by those with a legal capacity to contract. The most familiar limit on legal capacity to contract is age; other limitations include mental disability and intoxication. Usually when a contract is made by someone without the legal capacity to do so, that person has the right to decide whether the contract shall be validated when he becomes legally capable (old enough, sober, etc.) to do so. The point of this rule is to prevent people from getting into situations they are not mature or stable enough to handle.

Assuming the parties have legal capacity, they negotiate until they reach a "meeting of minds." This constitutes the contract. The negotiations normally take the form of offers and counteroffers until one is finally accepted. Over the years, this pattern of proposals and agreements has been carefully analyzed, and a set of rules has been developed to structure the exchange and make it legal. Most of these regulations are just common sense: both parties must be willing to contract, offers must be communicated and received by each party, offers lapse if they are not accepted in a reasonable period of time or if they are withdrawn, and so on. The main point is that the parties must show they want to make a contract and that they have agreed on the terms.

Even this agreement, though, is not enough. For a contract to be legally enforceable, there must be something called "consideration," which is essentially an exchange of values. An agreement that benefits only one party is not a contract, it is a gift, and is governed by different rules. Traditionally, "consideration" could be handled symbolically. One person could provide the other with payment of one dollar, or a peppercorn, as a token of exchange. More recently, courts have become skeptical of such formal "consideration" and have been insisting that all sides get some substantial gain from the contract.

We usually think of contracts as written documents, but this is not always so. An oral deal can be a legal contract. But spoken words are less precise and reliable than words on a piece of paper, and are more open to manipulation and cheating. So, as far back as 1677, the English Parliament created the Statute of Frauds, to require that certain types of contracts, such as those concerning the purchase of land, property distribution in a marriage, or any sale of goods worth more than a fixed amount (today usually five hundred dollars), be written. The statute also sets rules for written contracts more specific than those for contracts in general.

The Statute of Frauds seems like a very sensible policy and has become a basic part of our law. Like most laws, though, it can be, and has been, misused. Certain people have deliberately made illegitimate contracts in order to take advantage of unsophisticated dupes, who discovered too late that their "contract" was not a legal contract at all. Consequently, judges have been wary of the Statute of Frauds and have often stretched its interpretation to prevent it from turning into a statute *for* frauds.

But even if all the conditions of the Statute of Frauds and all the other rules are met, there are still a number of situations in which courts will refuse to enforce contracts. Certain contracts have simply been outlawed on the grounds that they are harmful to society. If a corporation bribes a congressman to vote a certain way on a bill, and the congressman double-crosses it, the corporation cannot sue him for breach of contract. Such contracts as those restraining trade, defrauding third parties, making bets, and the like, are legally null and void. Also, if events make fulfilling a contract impossible (for example, the painting to be sold is burned before the delivery), the contract will be nullified (although the purchaser can sometimes get his or her money back).

Finally, grossly unfair contracts may be unenforceable. Some contracts are termed "unconscionable"; that is, they are monstrously harsh or shocking, grossly one-sided, and hence void. Usually, one party agreed to the contract only under duress, physical or economic. Similar is a "contract of adhesion," in which the two contracting parties are of such unequal strength that one must accept a form contract prepared by the other if he is to get the goods or services he wants. In such instances, courts will often strike out particularly restrictive clauses in the contract without nullifying the contract as a whole. Our examination of the purchase of an auto will give an example of what some courts have held to be a contract of adhesion.

Although these rules for contracts are complicated and open to interpretation and dispute, most of the problems of contract law come not from the procedures for making contracts, or from assuming them to be legal, but from the contents of the agreements. Contracts are supposed to represent a meeting of minds, but people often find after they have signed a contract that the parties did not agree as completely as they had thought they had. Quarrels easily arise over what the terms of the contract actually mean, over what are the rights and obligations of the parties, over whether the contract has been adequately fulfilled. To meet these problems, the courts have developed rules for interpreting contracts, to supplement the rules on writing them. These rules deal with two basic areas: the meaning of the contract, and its performance. As far as meaning is concerned, the rules call for interpreting words in their usual sense unless there is technical language involved. When the wording is uncertain, the court will examine the context of the agreement. An obvious mistake in the contract (for example a typographical error) will simply be corrected. And handwritten entries have priority over typewritten material since printed items in a contract are often prepared by only one party without input from the other (as anyone who has ever signed a standardized form knows).

The purpose of having all these rules is not only to make it easier for judges to decide cases. If the people making the contract know how it will be interpreted in court, they are less likely to have to go to court in the first place. They will simply write the agreement very carefully, with the rules of interpretation in mind.

Similar questions arise regarding performance of the contract. In a simple deal—selling a pen for five dollars—there are no problems. But suppose a building company contracts to construct a skyscraper to certain specifications and meets all the conditions of the contract except that they used the wrong kind of water faucets. Is the whole contract void? Obviously, such a result would be unfair, and the law is not so rigid. The courts will demand only "substantial performance"; that is, the job is done basically right. Of course, the person who is paying for the building could demand a reduction in price for the faucets, but he cannot refuse the whole building for such a small mistake. Contract law, like most kinds of law, is more interested in making life easier for people than in entangling them in technicalities.

Suppose, however, that there has been a major breach in the contract, or that there has been no substantial performance. At this point the law will intervene, first to free the injured party from further performance of his part of the contract, and then to permit him to recover damages.

The basic theory behind the law of breach of contract is that the person who honors the contract should not suffer

for being law-abiding. An injured party may simply wish
to return to the status quo existing before the contract.
This is termed "rescinding" the contract, and it releases
the injured party from any further obligations. If the injured party has already performed his part of the bargain,
he can request "restitution"; that is, he gets his share
back. This approach would seem to be the simplest solution to the problem of a broken contract, but it is often
inappropriate or even impossible. For example, if a comedian contracts with a nightclub owner to perform two
shows for a certain amount of money and the owner with-
holds his check, the comedian can hardly go to court and
demand his jokes back. Other remedies, therefore, are
needed. The most usual course of action for such a person
is to sue for "compensatory damages." This device allows
him to make up the loss he suffered due to someone else's
violation of the contract. For example, if a wholesaler contracts with a farmer to buy one hundred bushels of potatoes for one hundred dollars, and ends up paying one
hundred fifty dollars to someone else when the farmer
fails to deliver, he can sue the farmer for the fifty dollars'
difference. When the injury is less easily measured in
monetary amounts, or when it does not arise immediately
out of the transaction but arises from later events, there
are problems. Thus, the wholesaler is offered a lucrative
five-year contract with a restaurant if he will only deliver
them some potatoes immediately, but he cannot. Are his
damages now the value of the sale to the restaurant or the
value of the five-year contract? Or even, perhaps, the value
of the new sales he would make as a result of the contracts
he would make with other restaurant owners, or the prestige of supplying this particular restaurant (which has a
world-famous French chef)? Here the fixing of compensatory damages becomes more difficult, and the law gets
detailed and complex.

Finally, in some cases, especially where no monetary
measure of damage is available, the court will order that

the party who has failed to fulfill the contract now do so. This is called "specific performance" and is used when some unique item is involved, such as a parcel of land or a work of art. Specific performance will not be granted where a contract for personal services of a human being is involved. To require one to perform such personal services would run counter to the Thirteenth Amendment, which, among other things, prohibits involuntary servitude: forcing one to perform against his or her will. This is why one who makes a contract to paint a person's home and then, improperly, refuses to do so, cannot be forced to paint the house under the principle of "specific performance." The recalcitrant painter will have to be dealt with in another way, e.g. compensatory damages.

Remedies like these are also available in cases in which no formal contract was made. Sometimes situations arise in which one person provides another with a valuable good or service without having secured a contract first. In such cases, the courts will declare that a "quasi contract" exists, and require some compensation for the worker or seller. For instance, a homeowner discusses with a painter the possibility of having his house painted. No contract is made, not even an oral one, but the painter reasonably assumes that he should paint the house while the owner is on vacation. If the job is satisfactory, a court may declare a quasi contract exists and compel the owner to pay a fair amount for the job. The theory behind the law is that it would be unfair for one party to gain unjust enrichment at the expense of another. Of course, the painter's actions had to be reasonable; he cannot simply go through the neighborhood painting houses and then demanding payment on the grounds of a quasi contract.

Legal remedies are also used in cases in which no contract exists, but in which it is understood that payment is required. If a patient goes into a doctor's office and receives a physical examination, he cannot claim afterward that since no contract was reached between him and the doctor, he does not have to pay the bill. That is the kind of argument that people who know nothing about the law call "legalistic," but no court would accept it. Contract law, like all law, is very far from perfect, but it does exhibit common sense. It tries, within its limitations, to make agreements and transactions as simple and as fair as possible. An examination in detail of a typical contract will show how the law works out in practice.

Purchase of an Automobile

Most of us either have bought or someday will buy a car. Except for buying a house, it is the most expensive transaction in which most people ever take part. And it involves, almost always, a written contract.

The contract we will study will be for the purchase of a vehicle from a regular auto dealer. Typically in such a sale, most of the bargaining and offers center on price: the price of the car, the price of a trade-in, and so on. The other aspects of the agreement are not normally subject to negotiation. These conditions are insisted upon by the dealer, and it is almost impossible to find a dealer willing to sell a new car without these conditions. Thus, the buyer is faced with something that looks like a "contract of adhesion." The following contract is fairly typical.

Date_____

Purchaser's Name_____

Purchaser's Address_____

_____

Magna Motors
1215 Charter Street
Runnymede
PLEASE ENTER MY ORDER FOR THE FOLLOWING:
___New or ___Used   ___Car or___Truck
Year_____Make_____Model_____Type_____Color_____
Serial Number_____To be delivered on or about_____

Insurance	Amount	Term	Premium Cost
Fire and Theft			

Collision
Public Liability
Property Damage
Credit Life
Name of Insurer_____
Address of Insurer_____
Cash Price of Car........................$_____
Options_____ .... _____
_____ .... _____
_____ .... _____
_____ .... _____
Total .... _____
Tax .... _____
1. Total cash price delivered.............. _____
2. Down payment...................... _____
3. Unpaid balance of cash price (1 − 2)..... _____
4. Finance charge...................... _____
5. Total of payments (3 + 4)............. _____
6. Annual percentage rate................. _____%
Finance charges begin to accrue on _____. The total of
payments shall be repaid to _____ in ____ consecutive
monthly installments of $_____ each on the ____ day of each
month commencing _____ plus one final installment of
$_____ due _____. If final monthly installment is
more than twice amount of an otherwise regularly scheduled equal
payment, balloon payment in amount of $_____ is due on
_____. Balloon payment shall be paid when due and may
not be refinanced. If any installment is in default more than 10
days, default charges shall be payable in the amount of ____%
of the delinquent installment or $_____, whichever is less.
Seller shall have a security interest in the property until the total
of payments is paid in full.

It is further understood and agreed that the order is subject to
the following terms and conditions which have been mutually
agreed upon:

1. The manufacturer has reserved the right to change the list
price of new motor vehicles without notice and in the event that
the list price of the new car ordered hereunder is so changed, the
cash delivered price, which is based on list price effective on the
day of delivery, will govern in this transaction. But if such cash

delivered price is increased the purchaser may, if dissatisfied with such increased price, cancel this order, in which event if a used car has been traded in as a part of the consideration herein, such used car shall be returned to the purchaser upon payment of a reasonable charge for storage and repairs (if any) or, if the used car has been previously sold by the dealer, the amount received therefor, less a selling commission of 15% and any expense incurred in storing, insuring, conditioning or advertising said car for sale, shall be returned to the purchaser.

2. If the used car is not to be delivered to the dealer until delivery of the new car, the used car shall be reappraised at that time and such reappraisal value shall determine the allowance made for such used car. The purchaser agrees to deliver the original bill of sale and the title to any used car traded herein along with the delivery of such car, and the purchaser warrants such used car to be his property free and clear of all liens and encumbrances except as otherwise noted herein.

3. Upon the failure or refusal of the purchaser to complete said purchase for any reason other than cancellation on account of increase in price, the cash deposit may be retained as liquidated damages, and in the event a used car has been taken in trade, the purchaser hereby authorizes dealer to sell said used car, and the dealer shall be entitled to reimburse himself out of the proceeds of such sale for the expenses specified in paragraph (1) above and also for his expenses and losses incurred or suffered as the result of purchaser's failure to complete said purchase.

4. The manufacturer has the right to make any changes in the model or design of any accessories and part of any new motor vehicle at any time without creating any obligation on the part of either the dealer or the manufacturer to make corresponding changes in the car covered by this order either before or subsequent to the delivery of such car to the purchaser.

5. Dealer shall not be liable for delays caused by the manufacturer, accidents, strikes, fires, or other causes beyond the control of the dealer.

6. The price of the car quoted herein does not include any tax or taxes imposed by any governmental authority prior to or at the time of delivery of such car unless expressly so stated, but the purchaser assumes and agrees to pay, unless prohibited by law, any taxes, except income taxes, imposed on or incidental to the trans-

action herein, regardless of the person having the primary tax liability.

7. It is expressly agreed that there are no warranties, express or implied, made by either the selling dealer or the manufacturer on the motor vehicle, chassis or parts furnished hereunder except, in the case of a new motor vehicle, the warranty expressly given to the purchaser upon the delivery of such motor vehicle or chassis. The selling dealer also agrees to promptly perform and fulfill all terms and conditions of the owner service policy.

8. In the event that the transaction referred to in this order is not a cash transaction, the purchaser herein, before or at the time of delivery of the car ordered, and in accordance with the terms and conditions of payment indicated in this order, will execute a chattel mortgage, conditional sales contract, or such other form of agreement as may be indicated in this order.

9. In case the car covered by this order is a used car, no warranty or representation is made as to the extent such car has been used, regardless of the mileage shown on the speedometer of said used car.

10. Purchaser agrees that this order includes all of the terms and conditions listed herein, that this order cancels and supersedes any prior agreement and as of the date hereof comprises the complete and exclusive statement of the terms of the agreement relating to the subject matters covered hereby, and that this order shall not become binding until accepted by dealer and in the event of a time sale, dealer shall not be obligated to sell until approval of the terms hereof is given by a bank or finance company willing to purchase a retail installment contract between the parties hereto based on such terms.

11. Purchaser by his/her execution of this order certifies that he/she is 21 years of age or older and acknowledges that he/she has read its terms and conditions and has received a true copy of this order.

Purchaser's Signature_____

Dealer's Signature_____

As in any transaction involving a contract, the first step is to read the document carefully. Some points stand out immediately. First, this is a *written* contract. That is be-

cause the Statute of Frauds requires that a written contract
be used in sales of over five hundred dollars. At its start,
the contract identifies the parties, both seller (Magna
Motors) and buyer. The manufacturer's name does not appear, for he is not, strictly speaking, a party to the contract.
Nevertheless, since the manufacturer obviously has a stake
in auto sales, and since he is mentioned in the contract
from time to time, in many states he is regarded as a
"beneficiary" of the contract, which gives him rights and
obligations too. At the end of the agreement, in item (11),
the purchaser must certify that he is twenty-one years old,
which means he has the "legal capacity" to contract. This
does *not* mean that people under twenty-one can go around
signing contracts without having to worry about having to
go through with them: in some states the purchase of a
car is an exception to the rule that contracts by people
under twenty-one are not binding, or a court may rule a
youth had the capacity to make the contract in spite of
age, most commonly if he or she is married, has a family,
or is employed.

The contract, of course, specifies the subject matter of
the agreement: the car and its price. It has a list of clauses
dealing with insurance coverage and financing arrangements, a set of conditions governing the transaction, and,
finally, lines for signatures. Naturally, no one is bound by
the contract until he has signed it.

Conditions (1) through (9) deserve special notice. They
deal with such possible problems as a change in the list
price of the car, changes in style, delays in delivery, and
so on. The ostensible purpose of these clauses is to foresee problems that may arise and provide in advance for
their resolution. But they are also heavily weighted in favor
of the dealer and the manufacturer. Reading these clauses,
we notice how often the dealer or manufacturer is relieved
of responsibility, and how often the purchaser must assume
it. Item (7) is perhaps the most troublesome of all. It
asserts that the dealer accepts no responsibility for the per-

formance of the car beyond what is specified in the warranty. In general, these warranties are for a limited time (e.g., one year or twelve thousand miles), do not cover injuries that may result from failure of the car, and do not even guarantee that the car will run. This clause is so unfair that courts in many states will not enforce it. But the dealer will almost always refuse to make any changes in the contract.

Often a buyer will also sign a second contract, this time with a bank or lending company, to finance the purchase of the car. Usually, the contract resembles the one for the original transaction, but with some added clauses. Let us look at a sample set of these additional provisions.

Terms and Conditions

1. Buyer(s) acknowledge(s) motive of Seller's intended assignment of this contract to [the financial institution] (hereinafter called the "Assignee"), request(s) the Assignee to acquire the same and agree(s) not to assert against the Assignee any claim or defense arising out of the sale described herein, and that upon such assignment, the Assignee shall thereupon be free from any claims or defenses which Buyer(s) may have against Seller.

2. Buyer(s) agree(s): to keep Motor Vehicle free from liens; not to sell, transfer or encumber same, not to use it illegally; and not to remove said Motor Vehicle from the county where Buyer(s) now reside(s) as above stated, without the written consent of the holder of this Contract (hereinafter called the "Holder"), except for temporary uses for periods not in excess of thirty days; that loss, damage or destruction of said Motor Vehicle shall not release Buyer(s) from payment hereunder; that any notices to Buyer(s) shall be given to Buyer(s) at his (their) address(es) set forth above. Buyer(s) warrant(s) that any motor vehicle traded in as part of the purchase price herein is not subject to any lien or encumbrance and any breach of said warranty shall be a breach of this Contract.

3. Buyer(s) agree(s) that time is of the essence of this Contract, and if Buyer(s) shall make default in the payment of the Total of Payments as shown on the reverse side hereof, or any part thereof, either on the due date thereof or when the same

becomes due prior thereto as provided herein, or if Buyer(s) shall
be adjudicated a bankrupt or take advantage of any insolvency
law, or if any judgment shall be taken against Buyer(s), or if
Buyer(s) shall make an assignment for the benefit of creditors,
or shall violate or fail to fulfill or comply with any one or more
of the covenants and agreements herein contained, or in case
Holder shall at any time for reasonable cause feel itself unsafe
or the Motor Vehicle in jeopardy, or in case of loss or damage
to the Motor Vehicle, then, and in any of said events, the entire
amount unpaid upon the Total of Payments as shown on the
reverse side hereof shall become immediately due and payable,
and, in addition, there shall be due and payable an attorney's
fee of 15% of said unpaid amount, if this Contract is referred to an attorney, plus court costs, and the Holder shall thereupon be entitled to and may take immediate possession of and
remove the Motor Vehicle and, as bailee for the benefit of
Buyer(s), any articles therein, without demand for the possession
thereof and without notice to Buyer(s) and sell the same at one
or more private sales or one or more public sales and, if sold
at public sale, purchase the same in the same manner and to
the same extent as a person not interested therein and hold the
same thereafter in its own right absolutely free from any claims
whatsoever; that Buyer(s) agree(s) to pay the deficiency as determined in accordance with law.

4. Buyer(s) will, within five days after repossession, notify
Holder by registered mail as to all articles claimed to have been
in the Motor Vehicle at the time of its repossession and will
call for such articles within seven days after being notified by
Holder by mail as to where such articles may be called for; otherwise, Buyer(s) will be deemed to have abandoned such articles.

5. Buyer(s) further agree(s): that any extensions or rearrange-
ments given Buyer(s) shall not be deemed a waiver or affect
any rights of Holder; that this Contract contains the entire agreement between the parties and that no guaranty or warranty, either
express or implied, not expressly stated herein shall limit or qualify
this Contract; and that the provisions of this Contract are severa-
ble and the invalidity of any of them shall not affect the remaining provisions. Buyer(s) authorize(s) Holder to file a financing
statement relating to this Contract.

6. Unless Holder shall have procured automobile insurance and

an amount therefor is stated on the reverse side hereof to be included in the Total of Payments, Buyer(s) shall, forthwith upon the execution of this Contract, insure said Motor Vehicle and shall keep the same insured at all times against such loss and payable in such manner as the Holder shall, from time to time, require. Buyer(s) hereby assign(s) to Holder, its successors and assigns, any and all moneys which may become due and payable under any policy insuring the property covered by this Contract and direct(s) any such insurance company to make payment directly to Holder and authorize(s) Holder to apply such moneys in payment on account of any unpaid part of the Total of Payments, as shown on the reverse side hereof, whether or not due. Buyer(s) hereby irrevocably appoint(s) Holder as his (their) attorney-in-fact, with full power of substitution, to receive all such moneys, including the return of unearned premiums; to execute proofs of claim, to endorse drafts and other instruments for the payment of money, to execute releases, to negotiate settlements, to cancel any insurance referred to in this Contract, in the event of default by Buyer(s) hereunder, and to do all other things necessary and required to effect a settlement under any insurance policy.

Now, what does all this mean?

The first paragraph establishes an "assignment" of the contract. Under this procedure, the financial institution pays the auto dealer what is owed and takes over the dealer's role as recipient of the buyer's payments (plus financing charges and interest, of course).

The second paragraph requires the buyer to keep the car free of any other financial claims. The fifth paragraph contains a denial of warranty, and the sixth requires the buyer to insure the car. The key sections, though, are paragraphs three and four, dealing with default. Once again, we note how the contract is biased toward the lender and against the customer. Even keeping up with the payments may not be enough; if the financial institution (the "Holder") should ever "for reasonable cause *feel itself* unsafe or the Motor Vehicle in jeopardy," then it can call in the payments, plus legal expenses. (Of course, this feeling may be justified: the buyer may have recently entered the car in a demolition derby.) This situation is known as default by the buyer.

Once the contract is signed, all parties are obliged to carry out the bargain. A default in payment by the buyer would be considered a substantial breach of contract and would allow the lending company to take the car (usually called "repossession"). In fact, the lender does not even need a court order. He can simply send in a tow truck and pull the auto away, as long as he can do so peacefully. After repossession, the financial institution can sell the car and sue the original buyer if the price from the sale of the car is less than the amount the buyer owes.

The reverse situation can also occur. Sometimes, as everyone knows, the car does not live up to expectations. It may simply not work right, or parts may break down, and the dealer will not or cannot repair it. In short, the customer is stuck with a lemon. What can he do about it?

Of course, the first thing any intelligent buyer would do is consult a lawyer. The lawyer will tell the buyer that he has a number of remedies open. First, because the auto dealer has breached the contract, the buyer can attempt to cancel the deal. Within a "reasonable time" after the car is delivered (how long "reasonable" is depends on the circumstances, but it must be shortly after the defect is discovered), the buyer lets the dealer know that he intends to cancel the deal, and gives reasons. He returns the car to the dealer, cancels the registration, and makes no further use of or claim to the car. He then either asks the dealer for the money back (restitution) or for a replacement car (specific performance). If the dealer does not comply, the buyer goes to court. In the meantime, he pays all money owing on the car until a settlement or decision is reached.

Another tactic he might try is to sell the car. First, the dealer is notified of all defects in the car and given a reasonable opportunity to make repairs. If satisfactory repairs are not made, the buyer notifies the dealer that he intends to sell the car and sue the dealer to recover the monetary difference between what he paid for the car and what he can sell it for (less depreciation). The buyer must be careful to inform anyone interested in buying the car of all the defects in it that he has uncovered. After he has sold the car, he demands that the dealer make up the difference in price and goes to court if the dealer refuses to pay it voluntarily.

The third option is to keep the car, ask for repairs, and then sue the dealer to recover for the costs of repairs elsewhere, any personal injury arising from the car's malfunction, or other losses. In practice, any of these alternatives can take considerable time before a court decision is finally reached.

The process of purchasing an auto thus exhibits many of the basic attributes of contract law. However, the dealer and the lending agency both had lawyers at their disposal to help them draw up the agreements the buyer signed. This aspect of our example is not entirely typical. In reality, much of contract law concerns itself with sorting out the problems of people who made agreements on the phone, or by shaking hands, without an attorney at their elbows to advise them. The fact that the same contract instrument can be used in both types of situation demonstrates better than anything else the flexibility that has made contracts such a significant source of law.

6
The Lawmakers

Contracts are quite flexible, but their use is restricted to specific situations involving private exchanges. When a society as a whole, or whole classes of people within the society, are faced with broad policy questions, they most often turn to legislative bodies for the development of "statutory law." Enacted by legislatures, statutes are rules of conduct that can involve relations between private citizens, between citizens and the government, or between various government agencies. In general, these laws cover four major topics: the structure and procedure of government, public taxes and spending, regulation of private behavior (including contract law), and what might be called public behavior, such as crime, education, and so on.

The legislatures that produce state law are themselves a hodgepodge of senates, assemblies, town boards, and other sorts of elected bodies. In theory, their members represent the views and opinions of the areas for which they make the laws—hence the terms "representative government" and "government by the people." Most people realize, though, that this theory reflects reality only in part. In the first place, representatives are usually elected from a district within the region they govern, and therefore have to pay more attention to what their constituents want than to the good of the people as a whole. Then, in most elections the only way to win is to be the nominee of a political party, so the legislator must be careful not to alienate the party leaders. Finally, even if a representative were willing to follow the wishes of the voters and nothing else, he would soon find that most of the voters neither know nor care about many of the issues he confronts. He is thus forced to rely on the suggestions of special-interest groups, on the experience of other members of the legislature, or on his own beliefs and conscience. For better or worse, government by legislature is not much like government by public-opinion poll.

Legislative bodies themselves are organized in a variety of ways, but common to most of them is a fragmentation of power. Some of this power is in the hands of individuals, especially leaders of various types, committee chairpersons, party chiefs, presiding officers. Moreover, to deal with the innumerable proposals and issues that come before the more active bodies, most legislatures divide into committees, each with its own realm of specialization. Instead of having every idea come before the whole legislature for discussion, it is shunted to the appropriate committee, whose recommendation is always respected and often followed.

The effect of this decentralization of power is to reduce the speed at which legislatures act, and to encourage compromise in policy, since there are so many people who can demand a say in any law before it is passed. In addition, the U. S. Congress and all but one state legislature (Nebraska) are split into two houses, which means that every law has to be passed twice before it can be enacted. Thus, there are twice as many opportunities to stall a bill someone dislikes (and that says nothing about the veto power of the President or governor, except in North Carolina, where the governor has no such authority).

Nevertheless, laws do get passed. The process begins

with someone or some group writing up a proposed piece of legislation. This is called "drafting" a bill, and most large legislatures have professional employees who do nothing but help legislators draft their proposals correctly. From a purely technical standpoint, drafting is a very complex task, since the bill is going to be interpreted by outsiders, such as judges, and it will undoubtedly be applied in situations not foreseen by the persons drafting it. These difficulties, though, pale in comparison to the problem of rounding up enough support for the bill to get it through the legislature and enacted into law. By the time the committees, the individual leaders, and the legislature as a whole have gotten through with it, the bill has usually been modified from the original proposal to accommodate a variety of interests. Few bills escape the process of delay and compromise.

The laws that do get passed cover a wide range of subjects but share a common form. First, the statute is given a title. Next, there is an "enacting clause," which announces the intention of the legislature to make a law. The third part of the statute sets forth the content of the law in separately numbered or lettered sections. Often, this portion will include a set of definitions of terms in the law to help interpret it.

Statutes ordinarily have two other characteristics. In the first place, they are designed to meet a definite social need at a specific time. Once a law has been passed, it does not change by itself. Statutory laws do not grow. If conditions change, the legislature must amend or repeal the law to meet the new circumstances, or else the law will stand as an obstacle in the path of further social progress. Secondly, statutory laws are "prospective"; that is, they apply only to events that occur after they are passed (in contrast to court decisions, which apply to the past events that produced the lawsuit). This fact makes the passage of any law somewhat of a risk; the legislature can only hope that it has provided for all possible contingencies.

Passing a law does not guarantee that it will be effective. For the most part, statutory law is not self-enforcing, and the legislature normally seeks out a way of ensuring that the law will be carried out. Sometimes, the responsibility to enforce the law is placed in the hands of the public. For instance, the law permits contracts, but it leaves it up to private persons to decide what the terms of their contracts will be, and it is their job to go to court if they think the terms have been violated. Other laws more or less take care of themselves. When the government passes a law establishing welfare benefits, for example, or providing market information to businesses that request it, no one worries about punishing anyone who fails to take advantage of the offer. The whole point of government benefits is that they provide a service somebody wants.

Finally, sanctions may be used to enforce a law. We tend to think of sanctions in terms of prison sentences handed out to criminals arrested by the police, but these are only one aspect of the law-enforcement system. Administrative agencies, as we shall see, can be as vigorous in prosecuting wrongdoers as the police, although they tend to rely on economic penalties instead of jail terms. Depriving someone of a license to do business, forbidding a corporate merger, even public exposure can serve as devices to enforce legislative enactments.

Actually, the most widespread problem with legislative regulations is not enforcing them against evildoers but interpreting them so that people will know how to be law-abiding. The people who must apply the law—judges, bureaucrats, private citizens—are not the ones who made it, and so they may have difficulty understanding exactly what the legislature had in mind. This difficulty is compounded by the fact that the various persons involved in writing the law may not have agreed on what it meant either; the compromise process in most legislative bodies produces ambiguous and generalized phrases in place of precise legal wording. Furthermore, situations may arise that the lawmakers clearly never anticipated, but decisions must nevertheless be made. It is no wonder that courts have to spend so much time engaged in statutory interpretation.

The fundamental principle of statutory interpretation is to seek out the underlying purpose of the law. Identifying the purpose is especially important because many statutes use such words as "proper," "fair," and "reasonable," words with indefinite meanings that can be understood only in context. Therefore, reading a law requires not only an examination of the language of the measure but also an investigation of the context.

The context of a bill can be examined in two ways. First, the judge or other interpreter will attempt to discover what the relevant law was before the new statute was enacted. It is obvious that the legislature felt the old law was inadequate, or they would not have changed it. By looking closely at what parts of the old law were transformed and what parts were left intact, a judge can reason out just what the lawmakers had in mind.

Interpreters of the law have another aid in their search for meaning: legislative journals. Most major legislative bodies keep some sort of record of their proceedings, which not only records the actions they took but also the stages a bill went through, the amendments that were introduced (and which were passed), and even indication of the debate that took place when the bill was discussed. From these records the judge can draw up a "legislative history" of the law, sometimes including explicit statements by its sponsors of what their intentions were. Such information can be invaluable in legal interpretation, as our case study will demonstrate.

A Village Zoning Ordinance

The village of Beau Monde is less than a square mile in area and has about seven hundred fifty residents, who live almost exclusively in individual houses. The village has no business district and little traffic. Fifteen miles away, however, is situated the campus of a large university, and students have started to inquire about renting houses in Beau Monde, with five or six roommates planning to rent a single house. This prospect upsets the local inhabitants. Although they are not anti-student, they fear that an influx of college youths will increase the noise level and destroy the quiet family atmosphere in Beau Monde. So, like Americans everywhere, they turn to government for action.

Beau Monde is run by a village council composed of a mayor and four trustees, elected every two years. Among the powers granted them by the state legislature is the authority to regulate the kinds of buildings and business activities allowed in the village, i.e. the right to pass zoning ordinances.

The state law reads as follows:

For purpose of promoting the health, safety, morals, or the general welfare of the community, the board of trustees of a village is hereby empowered, by local law, to regulate and restrict the height, number of stories and size of buildings and other structures, the percentage of lot that may be occupied, the size of yards, courts, and other open spaces, the density of population, and the location and use of buildings, structures and land for trade, industry, residence or other purposes.

As laws go, this one is reasonably straightforward, but it is marked with that tendency toward repetition and long-windedness that many people associate with legal language. In fact, most of the specific wording developed from experiences in many parts of the country and is inserted to forestall problems and questions that have arisen elsewhere. For instance, the clause at the beginning of the law restricting the purposes for which regulation may be enacted is designed to prevent a village council from manipulating the zoning rules to make a profit for themselves (a situation that comes up from time to time).

In response to public outcry, then, the council requests that the village attorney draft a zoning ordinance that will restrict the use of dwellings in Beau Monde to families only. The attorney uses other, similar laws from other towns as the basis for his own text, and presents it to one of the trustees, who introduces it at a session of the council. There the bill is referred to the zoning committee (composed of the mayor and one trustee), which discusses it and recommends passage. The council holds a public hearing on the bill, at which some local residents speak in support, and then adopts it unanimously at the next regular council meeting. Thereafter the text of the ordinance is published in a local newspaper and a copy is posted in the village clerk's office, so that residents will know that the zoning rule has been passed.

The bill is in four sections, or articles. Article I provides a definition of the key term "family dwelling" in such a way as to exclude any place college students might try to live in.

ARTICLE I. DEFINITIONS

D-1.1a. One-family Dwelling. A detached house consisting of or intended to be occupied as a residence by one family only as family is hereinafter defined. In no case shall a lodging house, boarding house, fraternity house, sorority house or multiple dwelling be classified or construed as one-family.

D-1.2a. Family. One or more persons related by blood, adoption or marriage, living and cooking together as a single housekeeping unit, exclusive of household servants. A number of persons but not exceeding two (2) living and cooking together as a single housekeeping unit though not related by blood, adoption, or marriage shall be deemed to constitute a family.

Article II simply means that the ordinance will apply in the entire village.

ARTICLE II. DISTRICTS

DT-1.0. For the purpose of this Ordinance the Village of Beau Monde will consist of one (1) district, to be known as "A" Residence District.

DT-1.1. The boundary of said district is hereby established as identical to the Village boundaries.

DT-1.2. No building shall be erected, altered, or used and no premises shall be used for any other than a purpose permitted in this "A" residential zone.

Articles III and IV are the heart of the ordinance. The third article makes it illegal to construct any building in Beau Monde, or to use any building already there, except as a single-family dwelling. The article also makes exceptions for garages and municipal buildings. In case of violation, Article IV sets forth the penalty for disobedience.

ARTICLE III. "A" RESIDENCE DISTRICT

A-1.0. Within "A" Residence District no building or premise shall be used and no building shall hereafter be erected or altered except for one (1) or more of the following uses:

(1) One-family dwellings.

(2) Public parks, playgrounds, recreational areas, and real property and structures owned and operated by the municipality and for municipal purposes of the Village of Beau Monde.

(3) Accessory buildings, including one (1) private garage when situated on the same lot and when meeting requirements of Article III, Section A-1.4a, A-1.4b, and A-1.4c [another ordinance] and when such buildings are incidental to the principal use of the dwelling and do not include any activity commonly conducted as a business. The private garage may be within or attached to the dwelling.

ARTICLE IV. PENALTIES FOR VIOLATION

Each violation of the provisions of this Ordinance shall constitute disorderly conduct. The owner and lessee or tenant of the building where a violation occurs shall be a disorderly person and shall be liable for and pay a penalty not exceeding One Hundred Dollars ($100) or be imprisoned for a period not exceeding sixty (60) days or be both fined and imprisoned. A separate and distinct offense shall be deemed committed on each day during or on which a violation occurs or continues.

On the surface, the village council of Beau Monde seems to have drawn up a competent and comprehensive piece of legislation, and so they have. But, like most legislative acts, this one does not foresee all possible contingencies or apply in all conceivable situations. And, despite the included definitions, the law does need to be interpreted.

About a year after the passage of the ordinance a young couple, the Thompsons, purchase a home in Beau Monde. Although they already have two children of their own, they soon agree with a county child-care agency to provide temporary foster care to homeless young people. The agency thereupon sends them four children to take care of, and financial support. At this point, a neighbor makes a complaint to the village zoning inspector, arguing that the Thompsons are violating the zoning ordinance, since they have people living with them who are not members of their family (the statute exempted adopted children, but not foster children, in Article I). The inspector agrees with the neighbor, and reports to the village attorney, who brings the Thompsons to court.

It is now up to the village justice to determine if the Thompsons have broken the law. Reading the wording of the statute, the case appears clear: the foster children living with the Thompsons do not count as a single family as the law defines it. However, the judge is required to search out the purpose of the ordinance. He cannot, to be sure, rely on an analysis of past ordinances, because there are none, but he can look to the legislative history of the enactment. Examining the village records, the justice discovers that the intent of the regulation was to prevent an influx of students who might destroy the residential character of Beau Monde. The Thompsons and their children and foster children certainly do not represent an invasion by college students. Indeed, the whole idea of the foster-parent program is to provide homeless children with a family structure, the kind of family structure Beau Monde wants to preserve. In short, the ordinance was not really meant to apply to situations like this one. The village justice therefore dismisses the charges against them. It is the purpose of the law, he decides, not its particular wording, that is significant and binding.

7
The Courts

When most of us think about law, we find ourselves thinking about courts. We may recognize that many other groups and institutions share in the lawmaking process, but somehow the courts, with their careful procedure, conflicting lawyers, attentive juries, and learned judges, symbolize the majesty of the law better than any rivals. This respect, bordering on awe, for the judiciary developed only gradually and is far from universal. Even in the United States, some people shy away from courts; they regard the courts as serving only those who can afford expensive attorneys and long waits. This skepticism, indeed, has some basis in fact. Nevertheless, for all their faults, American courts represent an important human step toward justice for all, and the admiration they inspire is at least partly deserved.

Ruling over the court is a judge (or judges). We have already discussed the selection of judges, in Chapter 3. This selection process is so important precisely because, in the courtroom, the judge's power is next to absolute. In general, judges decide all questions in a case except "What happened?" "Who did it?" and if appropriate,

"How much compensation should be given?" This leaves the judge with the duties of maintaining order in the court, of ensuring that correct procedures are followed, and of interpreting disputed points of law. But in some cases, and in all appellate cases, judges decide everything, subject only to procedural considerations. Such powers can be quite dangerous when not used responsibly, hence the development of methods to remove judges (also discussed in Chapter 3).

Sharing the spotlight with the judge in court proceedings is the jury. In principle, a jury represents the considered views of the people, at least the people of the community in which the trial is taking place. The jurors are supposed to be disinterested observers deciding issues exclusively on the basis of evidence properly presented in court. Their collective wisdom, it is argued, results in fairer verdicts than even the most Solomonic of judges could achieve alone. To safeguard their impartiality, juries are led by the hand through the judicial process. Nothing that might mislead or inflame jurors is permitted in court. At the conclusion of a case, the judge carefully explains to the jury the law to be applied. Often the judge will go so far as to fashion precise questions for the jury to answer in its verdict. The jury then retires, in splendid isolation, to decide what happened, who did it, or how much compensation should be given.

The method of selecting jurors is also designed to ensure an unbiased judgment. Generally, people are selected for jury duty at random from voter registration lists or city directories. Once a list of potential jurors is completed, the court clerk or other official draws names by lot to form a jury panel. Prospective jurors are then questioned by the attorneys and/or by the judge until the proper number (usually six or twelve) is reached. This interrogation process—called *voir dire*—can be one of the most important parts of a trial. If, during the *voir dire*, a potential juror displays bias, the person is "excused," that is, not permitted to serve on this particular jury. Each attorney also can demand that an individual be dismissed without giving a reason; this is called a "peremptory challenge," and each lawyer is entitled to only a limited number of them per case. In practice, attorneys use their peremptory challenges to try to get not a merely impartial jury but a sympathetic one.

The very possibility of putting together a sympathetic jury has led some critics of the jury system to advocate its restriction or even abolition. Not only are juries ignorant, sentimental, and easily manipulated by a shrewd or theatrical counsel, they argue, but they are not even unbiased. Experienced trial attorneys have long believed that certain occupational, ethnic, or religious groups tend to react variously to the same set of facts. For instance, Scandinavian Lutherans are said to be unsympathetic to underdogs, while female Jewish schoolteachers are warm and friendly. More recently, professional psychologists have claimed to be able to determine a juror's unconscious prejudices by observing his reactions to certain delicate questions during the *voir dire*. If such techniques can be used to form a proconviction or proexoneration jury even before the evidence has been presented, is the jury system worth preserving?

Defenders of juries do not deny the reality of these phenomena, but they do question their significance. It is far from clear that either skilled attorneys or trained psychologists can really pick juries as neatly as they say they can. In any event, lawyers often claim an ability to "read" and manipulate a judge just as they do juries; yet no one suggests we abolish judgeships. In short, conclude supporters of juries, the jury system is as good as any other system of justice, and more appropriate to a democracy than the more professionalized alternatives.

The third group of important actors in the courtroom drama are the lawyers. Their role is of especial significance because of American reliance on the "adversary system of justice." In most judicial proceedings, the duty of presenting the facts of the case and the relevant laws is left not to an impartial judge or jury but to the parties. Each party tells the court its side of the story, explains why it feels aggrieved, and describes the actions it wants the court to take. With no more information than that provided it by these parties, the judge and/or jury proceed to make a determination. Naturally, rather than make their presentations themselves, most people hire professional advocates to present their version of events to the decision maker. Courts thus become arenas for combat between gladiators-at-law.

The adversary system is often contrasted with the civil-law system, in which the judge takes a more active part in discovering the truth. The differences should not be overdrawn. Even in civil-law systems, people are represented by attorneys, and our own approach has been modified by new rules that require parties to provide each other with vital information when so requested. Nevertheless, there is little doubt that the adversary system has produced a contest mentality in the law, a feeling that legal inquiry is a game between opposing players rather than a search for truth. Whether this attitude fosters or hinders the attainment of justice is an open question.

One point that everyone agrees on is that it is impossible to progress very far in court without a lawyer. Except in special courts (such as Small Claims Court), no one can master the procedural details without the guidance of an attorney. A system that demands representation by counsel is, of necessity, unresponsive to the needs of some people, especially the poor or ignorant. In effect, the court system bars the underprivileged, as well as those with novel legal problems that no lawyer wishes to handle. Efforts have been made to remedy this failing by developing government-sponsored legal-aid offices, public-defender systems, and similar devices. However, while the attorneys attached to such institutions are usually both competent and dedicated, the budgets are so small and the demand so great that they are inevitably inadequate.

The adversary system, and the consequent dominance of lawyers in the judicial system, has another unfortunate aspect: almost the entire court process is in the hands of attorneys. Schedules are arranged to enable them to take the time to prepare their cases, slowing down the entire system. Because the rules are tailored to the needs of counsel, it is extremely difficult for a lay party to determine how his case is progressing, or even what is going on. The decisions produced by judges are also aimed more to lawyers than to the lay public, thus doing little to explain the court process. As a result, some members of the general public have developed a distrust of lawyers and a feeling that the court system is being screened from their observation. As we shall see, the fact that much of the work of the court goes on behind the scenes does nothing to allay this unease.

Courts hear two types of cases: civil and criminal. While there are considerable differences between them, both kinds go through the same four stages. First, the case is brought to a court. Next is the "pretrial" stage, when, in fact, most cases are actually settled. If the pretrial stage does not end the case, it goes to trial, and then the court hands down its decision. We shall follow these steps in both types of disputes.

To begin a civil suit, the "plaintiff" (person bringing suit) must formally notify the "defendant" (person being sued) that he is being named in a specific lawsuit. This process, which follows specific rules and requires the presentation of legal papers to the defendant, is called "service of process." The rules are designed to ensure that the defendant will know what is going on, so that he can prepare his arguments. Thus, the plaintiff must usually try to serve the papers (called a "summons") directly on the defendant—"personal service." Only if that fails may he rely on "substitute service," e.g. leaving the papers at the defendant's home or business or, in very special circumstances, advertising in a newspaper. A court may refuse to accept a plaintiff's case if not enough was done to notify the defendant.

The summons states who the plaintiff and the defendant are, which court will handle the case, what the general issues are, and when the defendant must respond. If the defendant does not respond on time, the plaintiff wins a "default judgment." On the other hand, if the summons does not include all the necessary information, the court may refuse to accept the suit. Even at the beginning of the case, we see how important the rules are, and why people must rely on attorneys.

Along with the summons, or shortly thereafter, the plaintiff must "serve" the defendant with a "complaint" or "petition." This document gives a detailed analysis of the content of the case, a summary of the facts (as the plaintiff sees them), the relevant laws, and the relief or judgment the plaintiff seeks. Although the complaint can sometimes be amended later on in the case, normally everything the plaintiff intends to say must be presented, at least in summary, in the complaint. The document, therefore, is often long, and occasionally contradictory. After all, if there are, for instance, two precedents that say different things, the plaintiff might as well try to use both of them. One never knows which one the judge will consider relevant.

Once the plaintiff has completed his task, the turn of the defendant comes. The defendant may simply request the court to terminate the case immediately. This "motion to dismiss" will be granted if the court decides it does not have jurisdiction or if there is no way the plaintiff will be granted relief no matter how the argument progresses. Otherwise, the defendant must prepare an "answer," which either admits, denies, or claims ignorance of each of the plaintiff's allegations. After the specific points of the plaintiff have been dealt with, the defendant can present arguments of his own ("affirmative defense") and even make complaints of his own against the plaintiff ("counterclaims"). The exchange of complaint and answer provides each "litigant" (person engaged in litigation, i.e. parties to the case) with some idea of what the dispute is all about.

The next step is "discovery," a process permitting each litigant to gather evidence and ask questions of the adversary. Perhaps the chief mechanism used in discovery is the "deposition." In a deposition, a party or witness responds to oral questions put by a litigant's counsel. These answers are recorded and typed up for use at the trial. Written questions called "interrogatories" are also used. In addition, either party may demand to see relevant documents or physical evidence (such as a damaged automobile in a car-accident case) or even request the opponent be given a physical or mental examination (this last, in many states, requires court approval).

Armed with the evidence gathered by discovery, either side may make a "motion for summary judgment." This motion claims that there are no factual issues in dispute, and that, given the facts, only one decision is possible. If the court believes there are issues still to be resolved, the case is put on the court's calendar for trial.

With a criminal case, the process is rather different. A criminal case begins with the commission of a crime, or with the belief that a crime has been or is about to be committed. However, not all crimes lead to criminal cases. Police have a degree of leeway in deciding whether or not to enforce the law. This "police discretion" results from the fact that there are more criminal acts than there are enforcement agents; indeed, an entire police force could probably occupy itself doing nothing but enforcing parking and speeding laws. Moreover, much of a policeman's time is not spent on law enforcement, strictly speaking, but on community service: finding lost children, taking people to hospitals, and, of course, filing reports. Consequently, police must choose which laws to enforce under which circumstances. This discretion is inevitable when situations are ambiguous and the police have to make an on-the-spot decision whether or not to intervene.

Discretion, to be sure, can be either used or abused. Properly, discretion is used either when enforcement of a law diverts resources from more serious problems (arresting jaywalkers instead of burglars), or when justice and community welfare are better served by non-enforcement. For example, at the college at which one of the authors teaches, a village ordinance forbids parking after 3:00 P.M. This creates a problem for students on Tuesdays and Thursdays, when classes run from 2:00 to 3:15. When informed of this situation, the police chief replied that he could not ask his officers to ignore the law but that he would tell them to concentrate their activities on the other side of town between 3:00 and 3:30 on Tuesdays and Thursdays. This sort of policy seems only sensible.

Related to police discretion is "detention." Detention, which is distinct from arrest, involves the police stopping an individual for questioning in their investigation of criminal activity. If there is reason to believe the person being detained is armed, the police may "frisk" him, that is, pat the outer garments to check for weapons. If the frisk arouses further reasonable suspicions, the police may search the suspect for a hidden weapon. Often, a frisk leads to the discovery of some crime, e.g. possession of narcotics. Detention and frisking, on the other hand, can also be used by police simply to annoy someone they do not like; the discretion allowed to police officers can create great injustice in unethical or incompetent hands.

The criminal case itself begins with an arrest. A policeman may make an arrest either with a court order called a "warrant" or if he has seen a crime committed (in which case it would be foolish to require him to run to a judge instead of running after the suspect). In many states, the police may arrest a felony suspect even if they have not seen the crime if they have "probable cause" for their suspicions. Under common law, a private person who saw a crime being committed could make a "citizen's arrest," but this possibility has been limited by statute in most states. Such arrests are unwise anyway, since the citizen risks not only personal injury but a lawsuit if the arrest was unjustified.

May one resist an arrest? The common law permitted resistance to an *illegal* arrest, but several states have changed the rule, arguing that more harm may be done by resisting than by submitting. Resisting a legal arrest is everywhere a criminal offense, and the police may use force to overcome it.

For minor infractions, such as traffic violations, the arrest process is rarely employed. The usual arrangement is for the accused to receive a ticket calling for an appearance before a judge at a specified place and time. In law, a traffic ticket represents a summons by the court. The usual practice, however, is to require the person to pay a fine prescribed in the ticket. Nevertheless, he could appear before the court, on the basis of the summons, to challenge a police charge of traffic infraction. The entire case may be settled at that time. Often, the defendant may simply plead guilty by mail, in which case the judge will inform him by mail of the size of the fine to be paid. This proceeding is termed a "summary trial."

With more serious charges, a different procedure is required. An arresting officer is obliged to give a "Miranda warning" to any suspect who has been arrested. Named after the case in which the Supreme Court developed the rule, the Miranda warning informs the accused that he may remain silent and can call a lawyer (with one to be provided by the government if the accused cannot afford one). The purpose of this warning is to guarantee that poor, ignorant, or confused defendants will be aware of their rights, and thus to ensure fair play in the legal system. In fact, if the Miranda warning is not given properly so that the accused understands it (one cannot whisper the warning to a defendant who is hard of hearing, for instance), the court will usually dismiss the case. The law behind this is the "exclusionary rule." That rule requires that evidence obtained by police in violation of an individual's constitutional rights are excluded from a trial. The purpose is twofold: to preserve judicial integrity and to deter police from infringing on citizens' rights in crime investigation. In some situations, a guilty person might go free, which has led most policemen to be very careful in informing people of their rights.

The next step is the "booking," when the police record the arrest and charges. While the defendant is in custody, the police may gather certain types of information, by fingerprinting the accused, photographing him, taking a blood test, and so on. These activities are protected by the principle that they are evidence, not testimony (the Fifth Amendment forbids the government to compel anyone to testify against himself). The police must also bring the accused "promptly before a magistrate," usually within twenty-four to seventy-two hours, and the judge informs the accused of his rights and fixes "bail." Bail is a bond, a sum of money left with the court to guarantee that the defendant will return to stand trial. In some cases, no bail is required and the accused is released on his own or someone else's responsibility. Rarely, no bail is allowed and the accused must then remain in jail. The typical situation, though, is for the judge to set bail at some, but not an excessive, level. Generally, the two factors used by judges in setting bail are the severity of the charge and the likelihood that the individual will not leave the area. In other words, a local banker accused of littering will have a much lower bail than an international financier accused of embezzlement. Bail may be reset later in the proceedings.

Whether bail is met or not (if not, the accused must stay in jail), the case quickly moves on to the "preliminary hearing." The purpose of the preliminary hearing is for the prosecution to inform the court, by witnesses and evidence, of the nature of the case against the accused. The accused's lawyer can attempt to refute the prosecution's charges. Here the charge may be reduced or even dropped, should the magistrate decide there is simply not enough basis to go on to a trial. If the charge is not dropped, the court must determine if the accused should be formally charged.

What if the police fail to follow these procedures and try to keep the accused in custody without going to a judge? The defendant's attorney can apply to a judge for a "writ of habeas corpus," a court order requiring the police to produce the accused and inform the court why he is being held. Historically, this order has been of great significance in Anglo-American jurisprudence, and is labeled the "Great Writ" for its role in the fight against government tyranny. It does not, however, guarantee the accused his freedom. If the judge decides that the police have sufficient cause to hold the person, then back to jail he goes.

Formal charging uses one of two methods: indictment by grand jury or a bill of information. An indictment is like the complaint in a civil proceeding; that is, it informs the accused of the specifics of the charge against him. Again as in a complaint, all the points the prosecution hopes to make in the trial must be included in the indictment, so that the defendant may prepare his response. Normally, no new accusations may be added later. Indictments, therefore, tend to be lengthy and overprecise, as this specimen from Mark Twain and Charles Dudley Warner in *The Gilded Age* suggests:

The clerk then read the indictment, which was in the usual form. It charged Laura Hawkins, in effect, with the premeditated murder of George Selby, by shooting him with a pistol, with a revolver, shotgun, rifle, repeater, breach loader, cannon, six-shooter, with a gun or some other weapon; with killing him with a sling shot, a bludgeon, carving knife, bowie knife, pen-knife, rolling pin, car-hook, dagger, hairpin, with a hammer, with a screwdriver, with a nail, and with all other weapons whatsoever, at the Southern Hotel and in all other hotels and places wheresoever on the thirteenth day of March and all other days of the christian era whensoever.

This indictment must be voted by a "grand jury." A grand jury is a body of selected citizens, usually eighteen to twenty-three of them, who must decide if there is enough evidence against the accused to justify a trial. If so, they return a "true bill"; if not, they vote "no true bill" (this used to be called "We stand in ignoramus," but grand jurors too often took the phrase personally). Grand juries in some areas also serve as investigatory bodies, bringing forth recommendations for future action. In both roles, grand juries are typically guided by the prosecuting attorney and follow his recommendations. Indeed, the accused has no right to appear before the grand jury or to be represented there by counsel. Most states dispense with the grand-jury process in some or all cases and permit the prosecutor to indict by himself; this is known as a "bill of information."

The case is now ready for trial. However, in both civil and criminal cases, there is a gap between the conclusion of the preparatory steps and the actual opening of the argument in court—the pretrial stage. Faced with the actual possibility of pleading, and losing, their case, many people will seek an alternative. The opposing counsels, on behalf of their clients, will try to reach a settlement of the dispute acceptable to both of them. In a civil case, this is termed "settling out of court"; in a criminal case, it is called "plea bargaining."

These pretrial negotiations not only reduce the risk for litigants and save them time and money; they also reduce the workload of the courts. If every case brought to court actually came to trial, the system would probably collapse. Trials are long and expensive for the judiciary, too. Court space must be used; judges, jurors, and courtroom attendants must be paid; and none of these people can carry out their other duties while they are involved in a trial. Therefore, judges often press lawyers to persuade their clients to reach an agreement amicably, or at least without taking up the time of the system.

In civil cases, this operation is basically a matter of bargaining tactics. Each side estimates what the likely outcome of an actual trial would be, what the costs would be, and the risks of failure, and then proceeds to negotiate from that point. In fact, most cases are resolved in precisely this fashion.

Plea bargaining is a more controversial matter. Essentially, in a plea bargain, the defendant agrees to plead guilty, thus making a trial unnecessary, in exchange for a reduced charge. That is, a person accused of second-degree murder will agree to plead guilty to the lesser crime of manslaughter. Sometimes the charge is not reduced but the prosecuting attorney agrees to ask for a less severe sentence. The point is that both the defendant and the judiciary profit.

These pretrial negotiations raise serious problems of fairness, especially for individuals with limited financial resources. In a civil case, a litigant may be forced to settle for less than he really deserves, simply because he cannot afford to pursue the case all the way through the courts. The situation in criminal affairs is even worse. On the one hand, an innocent defendant, especially one who cannot afford a private attorney and is being aided by a public defender, may be pushed into pleading guilty by his overworked advocate, who will warn him that, even if innocent, he might be convicted just because his counsel must handle so many other cases at the same time that he cannot defend him properly. At the same time, guilty defendants often receive less than their deserts, simply by plea bargaining down the severity of the punishment. All parties agree the system is a travesty of justice; yet, given the limited personnel and money available, it is not easy to suggest anything much better.

If pretrial negotiations fail, the case proceeds to trial. Much of the procedure at trials is common to both civil and criminal proceedings. A court with proper jurisdiction takes the case, a jury with alternates (should one of the jurors be "excused" during the trial, e.g. for illness or for showing prejudice) is chosen, and the trial begins.

Usually a case begins with an opening statement by the plaintiff (his attorney, actually) or the prosecutor (in a criminal case). The opening statement outlines the charge or complaint and the factual evidence that will be presented to support the argument. The defense may then make its opening statement, explaining why its position is correct (or innocent), or it may wait until the plaintiff or prosecutor has finished his presentation of evidence. This presentation is the next order of business. Normally, evidence is produced by asking questions of witnesses: "direct examination." The defendant may then "cross-examine" the witness. A cross-examination centers on three aspects of a witness's testimony: Is it "competent"? (Is the witness able to observe, remember, and relate facts?) Is it complete? (The witness may have other information, favorable to the defendant, not brought out in direct examination.) Is it believable? (The witness may be biased against the defendant or may have given conflicting testimony elsewhere.) After cross-examination, the first attorney may wish to pursue some matters further through "redirect examination," which, in turn, permits "recross-examination."

The rules of evidence limit the types of proof that may be presented in court. The basic principle governing evidence is that it must be both "material" (related to a disputed fact) and "relevant" (it must prove something about the disputed issue). In addition, there are other restrictions. For instance, no one may testify merely based on personal opinion unless qualified as an expert in the field. Moreover, a witness can testify only from personal knowledge, not from what he may have heard others say (the "hearsay" rule, to which there are some exceptions). The thrust of these and other rules is to guarantee that only reliable facts will be used in reaching a decision.

When the plaintiff or prosecutor is done, he "rests his case." At that point, the defendant may ask the judge to dismiss the case on the grounds that the evidence presented has been insufficient to prove wrongdoing or liability on the part of the defendant. This "motion for a directed verdict" is rarely granted. Instead, the defendant presents his case just as the plaintiff or prosecutor did, with direct and cross-examination of witnesses. When the defense rests, the plaintiff or prosecutor may present a "rebuttal" and the defense a "counterrebuttal" and the testimony is finally ended. Each attorney then sums up his side of the story in a "closing argument" or "summation" addressed directly to the jury (or judge). Once the closing arguments are completed, the lawyers bow out and the decision is left in the hands of judge and jury.

The judge proceeds to explain to the jury the relevant law in the case. This "charge to the jury" enables the judge to summarize the argument and the points in dispute that the jury must resolve for itself. This charge must be prepared very carefully, since a higher court may overrule a verdict based on an improper charge by the judge. In fact, especially in civil cases, counsel may request that the judge include certain specific items in the charge. After having heard the charge, the jury retires to deliberate and reach its verdict.

In criminal trials, there are additional special rules to ensure due process of law. Most significant is the right to an attorney. A defendant in any criminal case who may face a jail sentence is entitled to legal counsel, and the court must appoint one if the defendant cannot afford one himself. If the defendant and the lawyer are not relating too well, the lawyer and/or the client may ask for a change. One defendant in a New York City trial (charged with mugging) was being represented by counsel who had been hired by the young man's family; the attorney was a well-known trial lawyer, slight of build and about sixty years of age. At the trial, the defendant suddenly leaped to his feet and twice punched his lawyer, knocking him to the floor. He then announced that he wanted a "mistrial" (that is, the trial should be canceled because its fairness was impaired), which the judge promptly granted. He also gave the defendant thirty days for "criminal contempt" of court, which occurs if someone's behavior is in disrespect of the court or when the conduct interferes with the administration of justice. The judge then appointed new counsel for the defendant. The new lawyer in the case weighed in at 250 pounds on a frame of six feet two inches!

A defendant is also guaranteed a speedy and public trial in an impartial setting. Speedy, of course, does not mean that the defendant is not given the time to prepare his defense. For example, in an Illinois case, a judge made a citizen's arrest of a former tenant at a house in which the judge owned an interest. When the police arrived, the judge convinced them that they should charge the person with theft, obtained a guilty plea, and sentenced the individual to eighty days in jail, all in twenty minutes. The Illinois Courts Commission removed the jurist for official misconduct. The purpose of ensuring a speedy trial is to prevent a person's remaining in suspense indefinitely. In addition, should the district be biased against the defendant (due, perhaps, to pretrial publicity—the interaction of a free press with fair trials is a vexed one), the defendant may have the trial moved to a new locality, a "change of venue." The U. S. Constitution provides still further rights for the defendant, including the right not to testify against himself, and other procedural guarantees. Finally, as we all know, no one can be found guilty unless his guilt has been proved "beyond a reasonable doubt."

Even after the jury has handed down its verdict, the losing side is not finished (except for a verdict of innocent in a criminal case). The losing side (either one in a civil case, the defendant in a criminal one) may request the judge to declare a mistrial due to procedural irregularities, or ask the judge to set aside the jury's verdict on the grounds that it is clearly indefensible, or, eventually, appeal to a higher court. In the meantime, the judge will direct that the jury's verdict be enforced or, in a criminal case, pass "sentence," that is, decide the punishment. In either situation, there are items worth observing.

In a civil case, the plaintiff has asked for a "remedy" of some sort, a response to his grievance. Perhaps the simplest kind of remedy involves a statement by a court of the rights and responsibilities of the litigants *before* any injury occurs: "declaratory actions." When, however, the injury has already occurred, different approaches are required. As we have seen (Chapter 2), common law allows *damages* (payment of money as compensation), while equity allows *specific performance* (an order to act to repair the injury). The amount of damages, though, is decided by the jury, if one sits in the case.

Although the prosecuting attorney may sometimes request a specific punishment in a criminal case, the final decision usually rests neither with him nor with the judge, but in the law itself. Some laws entail mandatory penalties, and these laws are binding. More often, the law sets minimum and maximum penalties, and leaves it to the judge or jury (depending on the state) to fix the precise bounds. A judge may also "suspend" sentence, i.e. not apply it, or put the condemned person on probation.

This judicial discretion in sentencing raises all sorts of problems of its own. For one thing, various judges have varying attitudes toward the crime. Some judges are very severe with property crimes; others are harsher with crimes against persons. Then again, some judges will hesitate to send first offenders to prison, on the grounds that people learn how to commit crimes in prison, not to repent for the one committed. Another judge will fear that, if first offenders are released, others will believe they, too, can commit "just one crime" and get away with it. These differences apply to parole boards also, and raise obvious questions about fairness and equal treatment.

Part of the reason for this disagreement among judges is the general inadequacy of our corrections system. In the first place, it is unclear just what prisons are supposed to do. Some want prisons to punish the guilty ("retribution"), others wish to prevent criminals from continuing their activities ("incapacitation"), some to discourage others from following their example ("deterrence"), while still others believe prisons should prepare inmates to return to normal life ("rehabilitation"). Naturally, it is impossible for prison officials to meet all these objectives simultaneously.

However, our current system of justice does not seem able to meet *any* of these goals. There is, for example, no good evidence that increasing the penalties for a crime reduces the numbers of people committing it, at least after an initial shock period. On the other hand, "recidivism"—repeated crimes by a former prison inmate—is on the increase in this country, to the point that almost three fourths of all crimes are committed by recidivists. Obviously, the prisons are not rehabilitating very many people. As for retribution and incapacitation, the diverse sentencing practices of judges and the impact of plea bargaining make achievement of either of these ends highly improbable. What is indisputable is that the rate of crime is going up.

Also unique to the criminal justice process is the "pardon." Historically in Anglo-Saxon law the chief of state (governor, president, or king) has had the power to grant mercy by relieving a convicted criminal of the penalties imposed on him. A pardon may be complete, or partial (reducing but not eliminating the punishment), absolute, or conditional (the person must agree to observe certain restrictions to receive the pardon). Although a pardon does not wipe the slate clean, as if no crime had ever been committed, it does restore the person's civil rights and remits the penalties. When a pardon is inappropriate, the chief executive may "commute" the sentence, that is, substitute a lesser penalty, or grant a "reprieve," a temporary postponement of the punishment. The idea behind all these devices is to permit flexibility in the criminal justice system to ensure the dominance of the most important part of that system: justice.

Whereas criminal cases mainly involve verdicts—determinations of guilt or innocence—civil cases not only settle disputes but also set precedents, examples for later courts to follow. We have seen that this reliance on precedent is a vital element of common law. In practice, the value of a case as precedent rests largely on the judicial "opinion," the written justification of the decision. Lower courts often produce opinions, and appellate courts do so in almost all cases. While the "judgment," technically, is nothing more than a verdict, stating the relief granted to the plaintiff, if any, the opinion explains the reasoning behind the judgment and the nature of the precedent the court wishes to set.

Opinions are typically divided into three parts. First, the opinion details the relevant facts of the dispute. After the facts have been recited, the court attempts to formulate in a short passage the basic issue that needs to be decided. Some cases, of course, present several issues, but judges prefer, whenever possible, to settle only one point at a time. Finally, the opinion recites the rationale for the judgment. This rationale usually includes reference to other precedents, as well as to statutes and principles involved. In addition to the court's opinion, it sometimes happens that one or more of the judges will write a "concurring" or a "dissenting" opinion. A judge writes a concurring opinion when he agrees with the judgment but not with the rationale behind it, while a dissenting opinion indicates disagreement over the judgment itself. Such opinions are important since later courts have occasionally adopted arguments originally presented in the concurrences and dissents.

Opinions, because they must provide a reasoned elaboration of the judge's views, tend to be rather dry and technical. Once in a while, though, a judge will get carried away either with eloquence or whimsey, and the results are generally worth reading. For instance, New Jersey Judge Harvey Smith encountered a case in which a defendant was charged with using obscene language to a court clerk when told he would be arrested if he failed to appear to answer a traffic violation. The judge decided that the constitutional protection of free speech shielded the defendant from prosecution, and said so in verse:

> Can you swear if you hit your thumb
> with a hammer
> Without risk of spending six months
> in the slammer?
> When the bank computer errs and
> bounces your checks
> Is your language confined to
> aw gees and oh hecks?
> Does the law require you to
> stand mute
> While a cigarette burns a hole
> in your suit?
> Is it reasonable to remain calm
> and composed
> If a photograph showed your
> horse had been nosed?
> Statutory attempts to regulate
> pure bluster
> Can't pass what is called
> constitutional muster.
> Use of vulgar words that may
> cause resentment

Is protected by the First
    Amendment.
There must be danger of breach
    of peace
For this near-sacred right ever
    to cease.
This was no obscene call from a
    sick, deranged stranger.
Of a breach of peace there was
    no danger.
Eugene hurls an expletive in
    sheer exasperation
And that isn't a crime anywhere
    in this nation.

Frivolous as such a decision may sound, its significance must not be overlooked. Judge Smith quite simply declared a local law unconstitutional, that is, unenforceable. Moreover, in our legal system, judicial opinions have a "retroactive effect." A rule announced by a court is usually treated as if it had always existed. Thus, a statement in an opinion can alter the meaning and validity of acts undertaken long before the lawsuit ever began. By his opinion, a judge can undermine rules upon which people have relied for centuries. The Supreme Court rulings on desegregation in the 1950s, for example, immediately transformed the policies of hundreds of school districts from legal to illegal (although the court did not require instant compliance with the decision). For the most part, judges hesitate before challenging established rules, precisely because of the impact their decisions may have.

How well does the court system work? Most of the rules that govern the courts are designed to ensure fair trials, and they pretty well achieve their purpose. Although there are exceptions, most cases are decided reasonably and honestly, if they come to trial. The real problem with the court system lies outside the trial process. To guarantee fairness, the courts have developed so many technical rules that it is possible to stall for months or even years before a case actually gets to trial. This slowness can itself be unjust, especially to litigants with limited funds or with pressing needs, who cannot afford to wait. They are thus at a disadvantage during the pretrial negotiations, in which most cases are actually disposed of. Combined with the heavy reliance on lawyers during the entire judicial process, this slowness has angered many private citizens, and discouraged still others. Clearly, not everyone is being properly served by the courts.

Still, not all the blame can be placed on the judicial system. Many problems in a society simply cannot be adequately dealt with in a courtroom. The settlement of disputes, the prevention of crime, the solution of family problems, and the myriad other matters that find their way into the judicial system inevitably overload it. Courts should be places only of last resort for a society. Until we find other ways to resolve our difficulties, the judiciary will never be able to perform satisfactorily and meet the demands made upon it.

Juvenile Crime

The court system does not ignore juveniles, but it does not treat them in the same way that it treats adults. Under common law, a child under seven could not commit a legal crime because of lack of *mens rea* (evil intent). A child, it was argued, did not know the difference between good and bad and therefore could not be held responsible for his actions. For children between seven and fourteen, the common law held that they could, in theory, possess *mens rea* but the prosecution had to prove it, as well as prove that they actually did the illegal action. Children over fourteen were considered adults for purposes of criminal law.

Over the course of American history, these rules were modified by statute, as people tried to handle the problem of juvenile crime. New York City, during the nineteenth century, deported young paupers to the West, while Illinois set up a special commission to hear cases of boys, but not girls, between six and seventeen. Toward the end of the century, a series of reformers persuaded states to adopt the rule that youths should be handled differently from adults. This principle still underlies juvenile law.

Each state differs on the details of its juvenile justice system, but we make some generalizations. A youth may be brought to the attention of the judicial system when the police catch him committing a crime, or his parents may complain that he is uncontrollable. In either case, instead of going to an ordinary criminal court, he is usually brought before a judge for a less formal hearing. The idea behind this approach is to protect the child from unfavorable publicity and to dispose of the case in a fashion that will rehabilitate the youth rather than punish him. Indeed, until the 1960s, the proceedings for juveniles were so informal that they were sometimes unfair. In one case, a fifteen-year-old boy was sentenced to remain in a state reform school until his majority (twenty-one) for making obscene phone calls; the maximum punishment for an adult committing the same crime was two months in jail and a fifty-dollar fine! The Supreme Court reversed the decision and declared that even in juvenile hearings some forms of due process of law must be followed. Juveniles, too, have a right to counsel and must be given the Miranda warning. However, special aspects of juvenile courts remain. For instance, a juvenile is not entitled to trial by jury, and most states avoid giving a youth an arrest record whenever possible. The goal is to achieve fairness without rigidity.

Juveniles have a special legal status in civil law, also. For instance, a student cannot be suspended from school without having the right to answer the charges made against him. Minors, as we have seen, are also restricted in their right to make contracts. In Connecticut, a seventeen-year-old won a state lottery of ten thousand dollars but could not collect because of his age. The state offered to refund his one-dollar ticket price. (Later, the legislature passed a law allowing him to collect the prize.) Most often, however, the special treatment of juveniles works for their benefit.

The real problem is not the odd lucky gambler, but juvenile crime in general. According to the FBI, about half of all arrests for violent crimes are of children under seventeen. Because juveniles do not receive the same punishments as adults for such crimes, the deterrence effect of the prisons is even weaker than it is for adults. At the same time, juvenile corrections homes—reform schools, industrial schools, and so on—are actually inferior to state prisons. Other factors, such as breakdown of neighborhoods and families, violence on television, and high rates of youthful unemployment, undoubtedly add to the situation. Whatever the cause of youthful crime, the system of dealing with it is under tremendous pressures and approaching the point of becoming at best a revolving door for juvenile recidivists. Many people involved in the system are giving up in despair. The Honorable Simeon Golar, former New York City Family Court judge, in his letter of resignation to New York City's mayor, said:

I have been especially pained to be part of a system that neither provides salutary punishment for delinquent juveniles nor offers any hope for effective rehabilitation . . . that with delay and a . . . lawyer [the youth] can beat the system. Thus, daily, we "graduate" juveniles to the adult criminal courts and lives of crime. It may be that the greatest contribution juvenile courts have made in America's cities for three generations has been to direct the occasionally delinquent sons and daughters of the immigrant poor from the adult criminal courts and jails. Happily, they were returned to communities where schools, settlement houses, churches, and synagogues, and lay and religious leadership provided opportunities for them to learn skills. . . . Today . . . we have abandoned the urban poor and their young . . . our schools fail to teach large numbers useful skills, and they drop out, and

This chart seeks to present a simple yet comprehensive view of the movement of cases through the criminal justice system. Procedures in individual jurisdictions may vary from the pattern shown here. The differing weights of line indicate the relative volumes of cases disposed of at various points in the system, but this is only suggestive since no nationwide data of this sort exists.

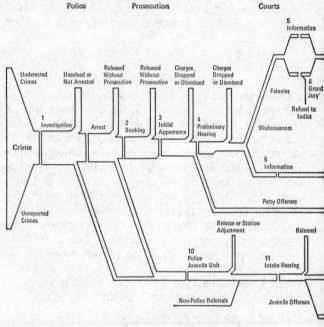

Police   Prosecution   Courts

1 May continue until trial.

2 Administrative record of arrest. First step at which temporary release on bail may be available.

3 Before magistrate, commissioner, or justice of peace. Formal notice of charge, advice of rights. Bail set. Summary trials for petty offenses usually conducted here without further processing.

4 Preliminary testing of evidence against defendant. Charge may be reduced. No separate preliminary hearing for misdemeanors in some systems.

5 Charge filed by prosecutor on basis of information submitted by police or citizens. Alternative to grand jury indictment; often used in felonies, almost always in misdemeanors.

6 Reviews whether Government evidence sufficient to justify trial. Some States have no grand jury system; others seldom use it.

7 Appearance for plea; defendant elects trial by judge or jury (if available); counsel for indigent usually appointed here in felonies. Often not at all in other cases.

8 Charge may be reduced at any time prior to trial in return for plea of guilty or for other reasons.

9 Challenge on constitutional grounds to legality of detention. May be sought at any point in process.

10 Police often hold informal hearings, dismiss or adjust many cases without further processing.

11 Probation officer decides desirability of further court action.

12 Welfare agency, social services, counselling, medical care, etc., for cases where adjudicatory handling not needed.

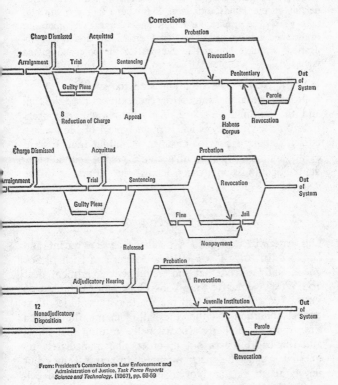

Corrections

Charge Dismissed Acquitted Probation

7 Arraignment Trial Sentencing Revocation Penitentiary Out of System

Guilty Pleas

8 Reduction of Charge Appeal 9 Habeas Corpus Parole Revocation

Charge Dismissed Acquitted Probation

Arraignment Trial Sentencing Revocation Out of System

Guilty Pleas

Fine Jail

Nonpayment

Released Probation

Adjudicatory Hearing Revocation Juvenile Institution Out of System

12 Nonadjudicatory Disposition Parole

Revocation

From: President's Commission on Law Enforcement and Administration of Justice. Task Force Report: Science and Technology. (1967), pp. 58-59 without jobs, learn to survive by hustling on our streets. Mr. Mayor, you have been properly concerned with our threatened default on our bonds and notes, but I hope that you will also raise your voice against our defaulting as a great city upon our historic social and moral obligations—particularly those special obligations we have honored in the past to the poor and to the young.

Sadly, New York's situation is all too typical.

No single example can convey the reality of both the civil and the criminal processes. We have chosen to concentrate on a civil case, which is more typical of the average citizen's affairs than, for instance, a murder trial. Instead of an example, we present a chart, prepared by a presidential commission, that details the criminal justice system.

Eviction Notice

Our case will deal with a conflict between tenant and landlord. In August 1974, Bessie Mieter and Richard Seigneur orally agreed that she would rent Apartment 6 at 100 West Avenue for $120 a month. When Mieter moved in, she soon discovered that the apartment was in less than perfect condition. Neither the bathroom nor the kitchen sink drained properly (occasionally causing flooding), and the bathtub was out of order. She immediately requested repairs. Seigneur promised to repair things but never did so. So, on November 1, Mieter informed Seigneur that she would pay no further rent until repairs were made.

On November 14, Mieter called the Department of Building and Property Conservation (DBPC) to complain about conditions in her apartment. The DBPC followed its usual procedure in such cases, sending out an inspector to examine the premises. The report, filed by Charles Checker, which included a long list of housing-code violations, is reproduced here.

DEPARTMENT OF BUILDING AND PROPERTY CONSERVATION
CITY PUBLIC SAFETY BUILDING
CIVIC CENTER PLAZA

NOTICE AND ORDER

Regarding Premises at: CR #752
100 West Avenue   Case No.   1000
_____   Extent of Inspection _____
_____   Date Issued   11/14/74

To: Mr. Richard Seigneur   _____
1 Main Street   _____
_____   _____
_____   _____

PLEASE TAKE NOTICE that an inspection of the above property, which is owned, operated, or occupied by you, has revealed that the property is in violation of the codes, laws, and ordinances of the City and the State and that the existence of these violations endangers the public health, safety, and welfare.

Included is a particular statement of the violations existing on the subject property, the state law or municipal ordinance which is being violated, and the time within which each violation must be corrected.

A reinspection of the subject property will be conducted upon the expiration of the time given to comply. If such inspection reveals non-compliance with this order, the Commissioner of Buildings and Property Conservation shall take whatever legal action is necessary to compel compliance with this order, or to cause the cited violations to be corrected and assess the costs of such action to you as prescribed by the Charter of the City.

ADDRESS   100 West Avenue   DATE ISSUED   11/14/74

HEARING RIGHTS: Section 52-5 (2) of the Municipal Code gives you the right to have an administrative hearing concerning the cited violations before the Commissioner of Buildings and Property Conservation or his representative. You may request this hearing in person, or by writing to the Commissioner of Buildings within fifteen (15) days of the date of this order. In the event you are given less than thirty (30) days to comply, you must make the request for a hearing within the time to comply.

If you have any questions, please call the Department of Buildings and Property Conservation.

BY ORDER OF THE COMMISSIONER

INSPECTOR ___Charles Checker___ _____

The following violations must be corrected within 30 days of issue:
1. Exterior trim requires protective covering.
2. Broken plaster in bath of Apt. #3, in need of repair or replacement.
3. Bath Apt. #4 lacks natural light and ventilation.
4. Doors into public halls lack self-closing devices.
5. Electrical outlets are in need of repair or replacement in kitchen of Apt. #3.
6. Electrical switches need repair or replacement in bath of Apt. #1.
7. Electrical switches/outlets lack covers in first bedroom and kitchen of Apt. #1.
8. Electrical switches/outlets lack covers in bath of Apt. #3.
9. Kitchen sink in Apt. #6 has illegal trap.
10. Kitchen sink in Apt. #1—faucets are leaking and/or unserviceable.
11. Bathroom in Apt. #6 is defective and/or leaking in Apt.
12. Beauty Parlor—Repair water closet to flush properly.
13. House drain in cellar has open lines, and water lines.
14. House drain in cellar has uncapped abandoned lines, and water lines.
15. Hot-water heater is improperly installed. (Apt. #3)
16. Hot-water heater lacks overflow pipe. (Apt. #3)
17. Hot-water heater lacks PTR valve. (One of four)

The following violation must be corrected within five days of issue:
18. Remove stoppage from traps and/or waste lines of washbasin and bathtub. (Apt. #6)

Permit must be obtained and work performed by licensed plumber for all plumbing work.

We note that the report allows for an appeal. In our next

section, on administrative agencies, we shall discuss this process.

Meanwhile, November and December went by and Mieter paid no rent. Seigneur, naturally, instructed his attorney to bring a lawsuit to collect the rent and remove Mieter from the apartment. In this state, as in many others, the City Court has jurisdiction over such cases. The attorney therefore drafted a summons and a complaint, and hired a process server to deliver the papers to Mieter, personally (personal service), at the apartment. When the process server handed the papers to Mieter, the suit officially began.

The first document, the summons, or "Notice of Petition," simply informs Mieter that she is being sued and must appear at court on January 9, 1975, to respond to the complaint.

CITY COURT

RICHARD SEIGNEUR
1 Main Street
        Petitioner,

   vs.   NOTICE OF PETITION
                                   TO RECOVER REAL
BESSIE MIETER   PROPERTY IN SUMMARY
                                   PROCEEDING
100 West Avenue, Apt. #6
         Respondent.

To Respondent BESSIE MIETER, the above-named person in possession or claiming possession of the premises more fully described in the Petition appended hereto:

TAKE NOTICE that a hearing will be held on the 9th day of January, 1975, at 9:30 o'clock in the forenoon of that day or as soon thereafter as counsel can be heard at the City Court at the Hall of Justice, Exchange Street, for a final judgment awarding to

Petitioner Seigneur the possession of the premises more fully described in the Petition and for such other and further relief as is demanded in the Petition.

TAKE FURTHER NOTICE that demand is made in the Petition for judgment against you, as respondent in the above-entitled action, for the sum of $240.00 with interest thereon from the first day of November, 1974.

TAKE FURTHER NOTICE that if you, as respondent in the above-entitled action, fail to interpose and establish any defense that you may have to the allegations of the Petition you may be precluded from asserting said defense or claim upon which it is based in any other proceeding or action.

Dated: January 2, 1975

_____

Lawrence Ford

Accompanying the notice of petition is the complaint.

CITY COURT

_____

RICHARD SEIGNEUR
1 Main Street
         Petitioner,

  vs.

BESSIE MIETER

100 West Avenue, Apt. #6
         Respondent.

PETITION TO RECOVER
POSSESSION OF REAL
PROPERTY FOR NON-
PAYMENT OF RENT

_____

Petitioner RICHARD SEIGNEUR alleges:

1. Petitioner is the owner of the premises known as 100 West Avenue, Apartment 6.

2. Respondent Bessie Mieter is the tenant of the said premises and entered into the rental and possession of said premises under an oral rental agreement made with Petitioner on or about the 30th day of August, 1974. Said oral rental agreement required

Respondent Mieter to pay Petitioner Seigneur the sum of $120 as rent each and every month on the first day of each month.

3. Respondent Mieter is now in possession of said premises.

4. Respondent Mieter has defaulted upon payment of the rental due and owing pursuant to the above-described rental agreement for the months of November 1974 and December 1974. Respondent Mieter has thereby defaulted in payments of rent due totaling $240.

5. After default occurred, Petitioner Seigneur duly demanded payment of said rent personally from Mieter and more than three days have elapsed since said demand.

6. Respondent Mieter holds over and continues in possession of said premises without the permission of Petitioner Seigneur after default upon payment of rent and due demand therefor.

WHEREFORE, Petitioner respectfully requests:

1. That a final judgment be made and entered awarding to Petitioner Seigneur possession of the above-described premises and that a warrant issue to remove Respondent Mieter from possession of said premises;

2. That a judgment for rent due and owing in the sum of $240 with interest from the first day of November, 1974, be entered against Respondent Mieter.

3. That Petitioner Seigneur be awarded his costs and disbursements from this proceeding and be granted such other and further relief as to this court may seem just and proper.

Dated: January 2, 1975

_____

             Richard Seigneur

Sworn to before me this
2nd day of January, 1975

_____

NOTARY PUBLIC

Mieter informed her attorney that she wanted to remain in the apartment and explained why she had refused to pay the rent. With this information, her lawyer prepared an Answer to the Complaint.

CITY COURT

RICHARD SEIGNEUR
1 Main Street
                    Petitioner-Landlord

    VS.   ANSWER

BESSIE MIETER

100 West Avenue, Apt. #6
                    Respondent-Tenant

The Respondent, BESSIE MIETER, answering the Petition herein alleges as follows:

1. Denies knowledge or information sufficient to form a belief as to the allegations contained in Paragraph "1" of the Petition.

2. Admits that she entered into possession of certain premises at 100 West Avenue, at a time and under conditions more fully set out below and is still in possession of said premises.

3. Denies both generally and specifically each and every other allegation contained in Paragraphs "2", "4", "5", and "6" of the Petition.

This first part of the answer responds directly to Seigneur's complaint. Mieter points out that she does not know whether Seigneur really owns the property or not (paragraph 1), admits that she is renting the place, but denies that she owes rent. The heart of her response, however, is her "Affirmative Defense."

FOR AN AFFIRMATIVE DEFENSE,
RESPONDENT ALLEGES:

4. On information and belief, Petitioner is the owner and landlord of a structure commonly known as 100 West Avenue.

5. During the month of August, 1974, an oral agreement for a month-to-month tenancy was entered into between the Petitioner and Respondent pursuant to which Respondent was to occupy one (1) apartment, #6, at that address.

6. The rent reserved to the Petitioner was to be in the amount of One Hundred Twenty Dollars ($120.00) per month, payable on the first day of each month.

7. Upon moving into the apartment, Respondent discovered that the sinks and tub in the bathroom and kitchen did not drain properly. If Respondent used the sinks or tub, they would overflow, making further use impossible.

8. Respondent notified the Petitioner immediately of the aforesaid defects upon discovery and demanded that he repair them.

9. Respondent on several later occasions demanded that the Petitioner repair the defects. Petitioner promised to do so, but repairs were never made.

10. Respondent, on or about November 1974, began to withhold the rent due because Petitioner had failed to repair the aforementioned defects.

11. On or about November 14, 1974, the Department of Buildings and Property Conservation (DBPC) inspected the property at 100 West Avenue and found numerous violations of the City Property Rehabilitation and Conservation Code, including those conditions which Respondent had complained of to Petitioner (a copy of the list of violations recorded by the DBPC is attached hereto and made a part hereof as Exhibit "A").

12. Despite numerous requests by Respondent, Petitioner has failed and refused to remedy the above-described conditions and has willfully and deliberately allowed the premises to remain in a condition dangerous to the health and well-being of Respondent, causing severe damage thereto, in that throughout the period of her tenancy she has been subjected to this degrading, unhealthy, and unlawful situation.

13. The above-described conditions constitute a danger to health, welfare, and safety, and as a result of such conditions the apartment is in violation of the Property Rehabilitation and Conservation Code.

14. The Petitioner has failed to comply with his statutory duty to keep said premises in a habitable condition, thereby breaching the Warranty of Habitability implicit in all residential leases entered into in the State, relieving Respondent of any obligations to pay rent allegedly due under said agreement.

WHEREFORE, Respondent prays that the Court render judgment for Respondent as follows:

1. That the Court deny Petitioner's claim for possession of the premises commonly known as 100 West Avenue.

2. That the Court deny Petitioner's claim for alleged unpaid

rent, in whole or in part because of Petitioner's breach of the
implied Warranty of Habitability.

3. That Respondent be awarded such other and further relief
as the Court may deem just and proper.

Dated: January 5, 1975

This particular trial will be a summary proceeding. Ac-
celerated procedures are not uncommon in landlord-tenant
disputes, as a quick determination allows rapid return of
the property to the landlord (if he wins) to rent it out
again and minimize financial loss. To speed up the process, virtually no discovery is allowed, and the right to a
jury trial is narrowly limited. In this case, the trial took
place in one day, just a week after the complaint was filed.

At 9:30 A.M. on January 9, 1975, the case of *Seigneur* v.
Mieter was called. The attorneys for both sides indicated
that they were ready to proceed, and neither demanded a
jury trial. At 2:00 P.M., when the trial itself was scheduled
to begin, the judge called the lawyers into his chambers
and pressed them to settle the case out of court. All efforts
at compromise failed. The judge and the attorneys then
returned to the courtroom, and the trial commenced.

As plaintiff, Seigneur presented his case first (that is, his
attorney presented it). He waived the right to an opening
statement, as did Mieter's lawyer. In fact, since there was
no jury and the judge had read the complaint and answer
himself, opening statements would have been useless. Instead, the attorney called Seigneur himself to the stand for
direct examination.

Seigneur testified that he owned Apartment 6 at 100
West Avenue, that he had rented it to Bessie Mieter in
August 1974 for $120 a month, and that she had not paid
the rent for November or December. His attorney then
asked him about the order issued by the DBPC to conduct
repairs. On the surface, this might seem like a hostile
question, but Seigneur and his attorney knew that it was
bound to come up, so they decided in advance to deal

with it themselves. Seigneur explained that he was making repairs as quickly as possible but was short of cash and could not complete so much work at once. The attorney asked how long he thought it would take to finish the repairs.

Before Seigneur could respond, Mieter's attorney intervened. His objection was based on the rule of evidence that only experts can give their opinions; other witnesses can testify just to their personal knowledge. Since Seigneur had made no claim to expertise in the field of apartment repair, his opinion was not admissible as evidence. The judge sustained the objection, and Seigneur's attorney said he had no further questions.

Mieter's lawyer proceeded to cross-examine Richard Seigneur. His first question dealt with Mieter's requests for repairs: Did Seigneur remember these requests? No, said Seigneur. This was a safe answer, since it is very difficult to prove that someone remembers something when he denies it. The lawyer tried another tack. Had Seigneur completed all the repairs ordered by the DBPC? Seigneur replied that he was doing the best he could. Since this was more of an evasion than an answer, Mieter's lawyer repeated the question, and Seigneur admitted that he had not finished making all the repairs. The lawyer asked him if he felt he had the right to disobey the housing code. Although the question was of doubtful propriety, Seigneur's attorney did not object, and Seigneur responded that he was trying his best within his means to meet the requirements of the code.

Mieter's lawyer said he had no further questions, and Seigneur's attorney "rested" (i.e. completed) his case. He believed there was no need to argue further. He had shown that Mieter owed rent and had not paid it. That, he believed, should be sufficient.

Mieter's lawyer moved that the judge dismiss Seigneur's complaint. Although the purpose of such motions is to save the court time, they are often based, as here, more on wishful thinking than on the merits of the case. Seigneur had clearly established a case, so the judge dismissed the motion and ordered Mieter to proceed.

Mieter's lawyer opened by calling Charles Checker of the DBPC. In response to questions, Checker described in detail the violations he had discovered during his inspection of the apartment building. The attorney asked him about the seriousness of the violations. They would make living in the premises "extremely unpleasant," he said, and added that some of the violations had resulted in a "five-day order" demanding almost immediate repairs. When he visited the building a second time, on December 19, 1974, he reported, many of the violations were still uncorrected.

Seigneur's attorney made two points on cross-examination. First, he asked Checker if he had returned to the apartment in the past two weeks. Checker said no. Were any of the defects or violations a direct danger to life or health? Again Checker said no. Seigneur's lawyer was finished with his cross-examination, and Mieter's lawyer called the next witness.

This witness was a realtor with extensive experience in the rental-housing market. First, the realtor detailed her credentials: ten years' work in the field, management of an apartment-locating service, membership in the National Organization of Realtors (Rental Section), and a graduate degree in business management. Mieter's attorney asked the judge to recognize her as an expert witness in fixing the value of rental property, and the judge agreed. Now that she was accepted as an expert, she could give her opinions on matters. Had she examined the property in question? Yes, she said, on December 2, 1974. What was her expert opinion on the rental value, in the absence of repairs? She answered that the apartment was worth no more than thirty dollars a month. Seigneur's lawyer, on cross-examination, asked her if she had seen the apartment in the past two weeks. She had not.

Finally Mieter herself took the stand. She testified that she had rented the premises, requested repairs, and had refused to pay rent. She described how she could not wash dishes or bathe her children for weeks at a time. Seigneur's attorney began his cross-examination. She admitted substantial progress had been made in the past two weeks toward fixing the apartment. Why had she not called a plumber to have repairs made herself? She could not afford it, she answered. Had Seigneur, when he rented her the apartment, promised to make repairs? She replied that he had made no such promise. Seigneur's lawyer ended his cross-examination, and Mieter's attorney rested his case.

At this point both lawyers made their closing arguments. Seigneur's attorney argued that there was no statute or precedent requiring a landlord to make repairs in an apartment or forfeit his rent. Mieter owed money and refused to pay. Under the circumstances, the judge should have no difficulty in deciding in Seigneur's favor. Mieter's attorney argued that the law was changing. True, there was an old rule against warranty of habitability (a "warranty of habitability" is a legal obligation to provide a decent dwelling), but the rule was more appropriate for times when most rental of land was for farming than for today. Many states had already made the change, and this state should follow suit.

Clearly, the issue here was one of law. Both sides agreed on the basic facts, but they disagreed about the proper judgment. In particular, they disagreed about the notion of an implied warrant of habitability. The judge requested each attorney to prepare a brief just on this issue, and then proceeded to consider his decision.

After review of the briefs, and extensive research and analysis of his own, the judge concluded that Mieter was in the right. He therefore prepared an opinion providing a reasoned justification of his decision. First, he gives a short statement of the issue in dispute.

RICHARD SEIGNEUR, Petitioner v. BESSIE MIETER,
Respondent

CITY COURT

Thomas Katt, Judge. The court is called upon to determine
whether a warranty of habitability should be implied in the rental
of residential premises.

Next, he reviews the facts of the case.

THE FACTS

Petitioner Seigneur rented Apartment #6 at 100 West Avenue to Respondent Mieter on August 30, 1974, for a monthly
rental of $120. Shortly thereafter respondent discovered that sinks
in the bathroom and kitchen and the tub in the bathroom of
the apartment did not function properly. Respondent requested
that petitioner make repairs. No repairs were made, and on November 1, 1974, respondent began to withhold rent.

On November 14, 1974, Charles Checker of the Department
of Buildings and Property Conservation (DBPC) inspected the
building at 100 West Avenue. His inspection uncovered a number
of violations of the Property Rehabilitation and Conservation
Code including the conditions about which respondent had complained to petitioner. The DBPC issued an order mandating repairs. Checker reinspected the premises on December 19, 1974,
and found that repairs had not been made.

This proceeding was commenced in January 1975 to collect
rent allegedly owing for the months of November and December
1974 and for a warrant of eviction. The respondent asserted an
affirmative defense based upon the theory that all residential
leases in this state include an implied warranty of habitability.
Trial was held on January 9, 1975. At trial, evidence was adduced
that the market rental value of the premises at 100 West Avenue was approximately $30 per month while the sinks and tubs
were out of repair. Petitioner argues that no warranty of habitability should be implied in a lease of residential property and
that he is entitled to recover rent and obtain a warrant of eviction.

Then the judge goes on to analyze the legal issue. He
begins by quoting from the earlier cases which denied that

any warranty of habitability existed. The opinions in
O'Brien v. *Capwell* and *Daly* v. *Wise* (the numbers and
letters in parentheses refer to the source of the opinion—
we explain them in the annotated bibliography) are especially relevant.

THE LAW

It has long been the law in this State, following common-
law principles, that there is no implied warranty of habitability
in a rental property. In *O'Brien* v. *Capwell* (59 Barb. 497, 504)
it was stated: "As between landlord and tenant when there is
no fraud or false representations or deceit, and in the absence
of an express warranty or covenant to repair, there is no implied
covenant that the demised premises are suitable or fit for occupa-
tion, or for the particular use which the tenant intends to make
of them, or that they are in a safe condition for use; and that
the principle of *caveat emptor* applied to all contracts for the letting of property, real, personal, or mixed as much as to contracts
of sale." In *Daly* v. *Wise* (132 NY 306, 309–310) the court
said: "In case the whole of an unfurnished dwelling is leased
for a definite term, under a single contract which contains no
covenant that the premises are in good repair, or that the lessor
will put or keep them so, the law does not imply a covenant
on the part of the lessor that the dwelling is without inherent
defects rendering it unfit for a residence."

But these cases date back to a time when most leases
were actually temporary sales of land for farming purposes.
In those days, renting land was paralleled to selling possessions—"chattel"—and the rule of *caveat emptor* (let the
buyer beware) prevailed. Leases, in fact, were termed
"chattels real" ("real" here means "immovable," as in
"real estate"). In modern times, however, this parallel is
no longer applicable. A lease is really more like a contract,
and both sides have obligations.

The judge bolsters his argument with references to
other authorities. He mentions two articles from scholarly
journals, one from the *Fordham Law Review*, one from
the *New York University Law Review*. In addition, he

notes parallel developments in the field of "products liability" and cites cases from other states whose courts had accepted the principle of warranty of habitability. Finally, he concludes by ruling that the principle of warranty of habitability is applicable in this case, and that Mieter owes only thirty dollars a month for the two months she skipped paying rent (minus court costs).

The rule laid down was promulgated in an agrarian society when leases were so much considered sales of the premises for the terms of the leases that the tenants' interests were termed "chattels real." Accordingly, once such an estate was conveyed, by lease, it was held that there were no further unexecuted acts to be performed by the landlord. Thus, absent fraud or misrepresentation, once the landlord delivered possession, the lessee would have no recourse against him should the premises prove to be uninhabitable.

It is evident that the rationale behind the common-law rule, which likened a lease to the sale of a chattel and therefore applied the ancient doctrine of *caveat emptor*, has no rational basis in a modern, urban society. Realistically viewed, and fiction discarded, a lease of residential premises establishes a contractual relationship with mutual obligations and is not intended to be treated as a conveyance of an interest in realty. The main concern of today's tenant is that he acquire premises which he can enjoy for living purposes; he is more mobile and generally less skilled at maintenance than the agrarian tenant; repairs are more costly, and dwellings, with modern plumbing and electrical facilities, are more complex. Thus, writers on the subject have supported the adoption of a rule of an implied warranty of habitability (see, e.g. 38 *Ford. L. Rev.* 225; 35 *N.Y.U.L. Rev.* 1279).

What was said in *Codling v. Paglia* (32 *N.Y. 2d* 330), in expanding the scope of products liability protection, applies with equal force here. The court there said (p. 339): "The dynamic growth of the law in this area has been a testimonial to the adaptability of our judicial system and its resilient capacity to respond to new developments. . . . A developing and more analytical sense of justice, as regards both the economics and the operational aspects of production and distribution, has imposed a heavier and heavier burden of responsibility on the manufacturer."

By a parity of reasoning, a warranty of habitability and fitness for the purpose intended (unless specifically excluded) should be implied from the very nature of a rental for residential purposes. This view is gaining limited or total acceptance in other jurisdictions (see *Javins* v. *First Nat. Realty Corp.*, 428 F. 2d 1071, *cert. den.* 400 U.S. 925; *Lemle* v. *Breeden*, 51 *Hawaii* 426, *supra*; *Lund* v. *MacArthur*, 51 *Hawaii* 473; *Marini* v. *Ireland*, 56 N.J. 130; *Mease* v. *Fox*, 200 N.W. 2d 791 (Iowa); *Green* v. *Superior Ct of City and County of San Francisco*, 10 *Cal.* 3d 616; *Kline* v. *Burns*, 111 N.H. 87).

Since "the law, as a living organism, does not require that the dead hand of the past perpetuate remediable errors" (*Sideman* v. *Guttman*, 38 A.D. 2d 420, 429), we relegate to the limbo of history the orthodox view of *caveat* lessee and hold that, unless expressly excepted, there is an implied warranty of habitability when a landlord leases premises for residential use.

Accordingly respondent's liability for rent during the months of November and December 1974 is reduced to $30 per month. Petitioner's request for a warrant of eviction is denied and respondent is ordered to pay to petitioner the sum of $60 less court costs and disbursements.

After the judge gave his decision, Seigneur's lawyer told him he could appeal. Seigneur, however, decided that the cost of appeal was greater than anything he might collect from Mieter even if he won, so he accepted the ruling. Mieter paid the sixty dollars (less court costs) and stayed in her apartment.

This case underlines the lawmaking function of the courts. As far as Bessie Mieter and Richard Seigneur were concerned, the central issue in the case was money. Once the judge had ruled that Mieter owed Seigneur only sixty dollars, their dispute was over. The true impact of the decision, however, came from the opinion, the *reason* for the decision. By accepting the claim of a warranty of habitability in rentals, the court completely changed the nature of landlord-tenant relations within its jurisdiction. It is typical of our legal system that such major shifts may be produced by such relatively minor arguments.

In one respect, this case is not typical of civil cases. The principles it lays down are real: the case is based on several genuine court decisions. In practice, though, such a far-reaching ruling is not usually produced in a single case. Instead, the concept of a warranty of habitability, or any new concept, develops gradually and is introduced only step by step into the law. Our case, then, is more dramatic than reality normally is. However, the process it describes does indeed reflect the workings of our judicial lawmakers.

8

Administrative Agencies

In one form or another, contracts, legislatures, and courts have been around a long time. Our last group of law-makers—administrative agencies—are a modern innovation. The first agency to play a significant role in the United States was the Interstate Commerce Commission, established by Congress in 1887 to regulate the transportation industry, particularly railroads. Since then, Congress and various state legislatures have created numerous agencies to regulate everything from electronic media to stock markets to labor-management relations. Indeed, the diversity of tasks they can perform is one of the most attractive features of these agencies.

The administrative agency is a hybrid institution. Typically, a legislature passes a statute defining in general terms the task the agency is supposed to undertake. The agency translates that outline into specific plans and ensures that the plans are carried out. Often, the agency will serve as the enforcer of the statute that created it, seeing to it that the rules are followed and disobedience punished. This role is especially important when private

citizens are too weak to protect their rights or when private enforcement of regulations is impossible.

The most fascinating aspect of agencies is that they
combine the lawmaking duties of both legislatures and
courts. On the one hand, agencies engage in rule making.
An agency may be charged, for instance, with planning
and overseeing major governmental and business activities.
However, the charge is too broad to serve as a guide to the
agency or to the institutions being supervised. The agency,
therefore, formulates regulations to flesh out the legislative
intent and make it applicable to specific day-to-day problems and transactions. On the other hand, agencies also
apply to individual cases the very rules they make. The administrative agency is the front-line forum to air and resolve conflicts among people in the area it regulates, or
even between people and the agency itself. When sitting
in judgment of its rules, the agency takes evidence, conducts a hearing, and writes an opinion, much like a court.
This adjudicatory function of agencies is as important as
their rule-making power.

If agencies actually behave like legislatures and courts,
why bother with them at all? Why not rely on the legislatures and courts to do their own work? In practice, administrative agencies have two advantages over their alternatives. First, agencies contain experts. Expert skills are
essential in resolving the complex technical problems that
arise in the numerous industries in this country. Obviously, no court or legislature can be expected to master the
vast amount of data needed to make intelligent decisions
in sophisticated technological fields. An agency, however,
because it is specialized itself, can develop and utilize the
necessary specialists.

Second, agencies are more efficient than courts or legislatures in dealing with small problems requiring immediate solution. Legislatures, of course, usually deal with
broad issues, and as we have seen, courts are designed to
guarantee fairness, rather than swiftness. It is impossible

for either to make the countless small decisions required
each day for our government to operate successfully. Agencies, though, are structured precisely to deal with the mass
of routine questions that need answering. Although agencies must follow some procedures, they have fewer formal
restrictions than legislatures or courts and thus can better
handle the mass of minor difficulties arising from private
and governmental activity. Agencies thus free courts and
legislatures for more important questions.

We shall begin with the agency as rule maker. When a
legislature creates an agency, it delegates certain powers
and responsibilities to that agency. All the agency's authority derives from that act of delegation. Hence, the
agency cannot stray from the path set out by the "ena-
bling legislation." Agency effort is, from the outset, narrowly channeled, and restricted to specific issues and disputes. Within its range, though, its authority is quite
considerable.

Because its rules can have an immense impact on those
it regulates, an administrative agency cannot do away with
all formalities in rule making. Agencies generally adhere to
a procedure allowing interested parties a chance for input.
Usually, rule making begins informally. Agency staff investigate an area to see if new regulation is needed, often consulting the groups involved. If they decide a rule is required,
they write up a first proposal.

The agency then distributes a "notice of intent to make
a new rule." Normally, the notice is published in appropriate periodicals (the federal government, for instance,
publishes daily the *Federal Register*, including all federal
agency notices) or other media. When certain groups have
a clear interest in the proceedings, the agency may notify
them directly. The notice contains the proposed rule and
specifies the time, place, and procedure the agency will use
in establishing a final rule. In addition, the notice
identifies the legal authority under which the agency is
acting.

The purpose of this notice is to give outside persons the opportunity to comment on the proposed rule before it goes into effect. This requirement of prior notice is critical to the rule-making process. Unlike legislatures, agencies do not have a free hand in fashioning rules. They must expose their work to public examination and deal with criticism before taking action. (In practice, legislatures tend to do the same, but they are not obliged to do so.)

The next step is for interested parties to submit evidence and arguments concerning the proposed rule. Although they are seldom required to, agencies often hold oral hearings. This commentary process is an informal one. The rules of evidence followed by courts are not applied, and the agency will consider any and all relevant material. It also keeps a record of the comments that have been submitted. While an agency need not change its proposed rule in response to outside suggestions, it cannot disregard these external reactions. Courts have the authority to nullify unreasonable acts by agencies, and the failure to consider reasonable criticisms is often evidence of unreasonableness.

After listening to comments, the agency is free to make its final rule. The rule, which contains a statement of purpose, legal basis, and actual text, must be published just as the proposed rule was. Obviously it is unfair to expect people to comply with a rule that has not been publicized. People can still petition the agency to change the rule, but such requests are seldom granted. In practice, the best appeal from an agency ruling is to a court.

This rule-making process takes time. Occasionally, an agency encounters an emergency situation, when it must produce a rule as quickly as possible. The agency, in such circumstances, can implement a new regulation without going through the normal hearing procedure. However, if an agency bypasses the initial notice of intent, it must permit comment and criticism *after* the rule has taken effect. This emergency technique is discouraged, and courts reviewing the rule will inquire carefully into the urgency of the situation.

The rules produced in this manner are much like legislative laws. Like statutes, they typically concern new problems, and remain useful only as long as conditions remain the same. They seldom contain any reasoned explanation or elaboration, but simply state the rule to be followed. Finally, like statutes, they are almost always "prospective," that is, they affect future conduct only. The most significant difference from statutes is that agency rules are "interstitial." Instead of setting down broad guidelines, agency rules fill in the gaps, supplying details not determined by the original legislation. Agency rules are as significant as legislative enactments, but they are, so to speak, smaller.

Adjudication is a much more formal process than rule making. Like a court, an agency operates on an adversary basis, with procedures designed to protect the rights of the parties involved. Agency hearings differ from courts, though, in that the agency itself is often involved in the case. Thus, the agency is in effect both defendant and judge in most cases. The difficulties that can arise from such a dual role are easily imagined, and the need for clear rules is manifest.

To carry out their tasks, agencies develop their own expertise. Whereas courts are totally dependent on litigants to present evidence, agency specialists will often rely on their own knowledge and experience, rather than outside comments. Agencies, therefore, unlike courts, can take independent action; they need not wait for someone to come to them with a complaint.

In taking their actions, however, agencies may injure outside parties. This occurs most often when an agency decides to cut off or reduce benefits it has been providing some party, either because the agency believes the party is not (or is no longer) eligible for the benefits or because the party has violated some agency rule. When an agency makes such a decision, it must notify the affected person in writing. The individual may then request a hearing. Once a request is properly made, the agency must hold a session to adjudicate the dispute, with the burden in most instances resting on the agency to justify its action.

The first formal step is a "notice of hearing," issued by the agency to the party complaining of the agency's decision. Basically, the notice resembles a court summons, specifying the time, place, and nature of the hearing, and the procedures to be followed. The contestant must be given a fair amount of time to prepare his case. Shortly afterward, the agency issues a summary of the issues to be aired at the hearing. The summary contains the facts and law that the agency is using to justify its actions. Since this summary notifies the challenging party of the reasons for the agency's decision, the agency cannot introduce new facts or legal theories at the hearing itself. The summary is thus comparable to a complaint in a judicial process.

The time from notice to hearing is usually short. While some adjudicatory proceedings require a written response from the complainant, this is unusual. Indeed, there is little opportunity for prehearing motions or discovery proceedings. Agency procedure is designed to emphasize speed.

Agency hearings are comparable to court trials, but they are usually shorter and less formal and complex. The most significant difference from a court is the presiding officer. In a court, the trial is conducted by an impartial judge; agency hearings are run by a "hearing officer," who is himself usually a member of the agency. The problem of bias is usually handled by separating hearing officers from other agency personnel (especially those who prosecute cases). Notwithstanding this precaution, many people have come away from agency hearings feeling that something less than justice has been done.

The hearing normally entails opening statements, direct and cross-examination of witnesses, and closing arguments.

All is done quickly and simply. As stated above, even the rules of evidence used in courts are relaxed in an effort to reach a quick settlement. When the hearing is over, the presiding officer prepares a written recommendation or initial decision, passing on all important questions of fact and law. This decision, along with the record of hearing, is passed up to the head of the agency. If he accepts the opinion, it becomes the final decision. If not, he writes his own opinion, covering the same ground, and that is the agency's ruling.

The law produced by agency adjudication is only partly like the law made by courts. Unlike court opinions, agency decisions seldom contain the kind of reasoned elaboration that enables judges to create common law. Indeed, agencies are not normally strictly bound to follow prior rulings. Adjudicatory law, in any case, is designed to resolve disputes between agency and citizen on a one-to-one basis, not to declare general principles. It seldom causes retroactive changes in established relations.

Nor does the administrative process have anything parallel to the elaborate hierarchy of appeals available in the court system. As we have seen, the only internal review of a decision is by the head of the agency (or someone he designates to deal with the job). This streamlined procedure makes possible consideration of a large number of cases in a relatively short period of time, and is implicitly based on the principle that a fast decision is more important than a correct one. In fact, for many matters, especially business dealings, this attitude makes a good deal of sense. The task of remedying injustice, meanwhile, has been left to the courts.

Agencies that administer statutes or rules are sometimes authorized to impose sanctions on violators. In general, the two powers available to agencies are to withhold agency benefits and to suspend or revoke licenses. The first of these penalties is imposed when an individual does not meet the qualifications for receiving the benefits the agency hands out (e.g. unemployment insurance, farm subsidies). Licenses are revoked when the holder of the license fails to meet the standards set for the licensed activity (e.g. flight route, shipping permit). In both situations, the individual concerned usually has the right to a hearing.

Certain agencies have other powers at their disposal: prohibiting certain actions, levying fines, collecting damage payments. However, agencies are rarely able to use these sanctions without the review of the judiciary. An agency may be authorized to order somebody to cease some action, but it is typically the courts who punish the recalcitrant. Generally, judges have been wary of agencies that assess fines, and they are ready to overrule such actions if the case so warrants.

Judicial review is the most significant restraint on agency action. Although the courts recognize the value of administrative agencies and have no wish to review every individual problem, they insist that agencies not engage in "arbitrary or capricious" behavior. Their review, therefore, is related less to the facts of the case than to the fairness of the procedure.

Courts, however, are not the only bodies with the power to restrain administrative agencies. If the legislature that established the agency, for instance, disapproves of the job the agency is doing, it can always change the law. The legislature also usually retains the power to fix the agency's budget, an easy method to discipline it. Finally, a legislature can always pass a law overruling an agency decision. (Since the agency derives its power from the legislative enactment, the legislature is its legal superior.) The chief executive of the state also usually (though not always) is legally superior to the agency, and may often have the authority to order the agency to do something or to remove some of its members and staff (this depends on the enacting legislation and civil-service status of the agency).

Moreover, the executive, too, is normally influential in budgetary matters.

Agencies, thus, are not all-powerful. However, we should not underestimate their impact. While in theory they can be disciplined, as a practical matter neither court, legislature, nor executive has the time or resources to oversee most agency activities. Any decision by an administrative agency may be overruled, but, realistically, most of their decisions are final. This fact makes their significance evident.

Welfare Payments

One of the agencies that gives out funds to individuals is the welfare agency. To qualify for public assistance, a person must conform to the statutory and agency regulations, including limits on income, property ownership, and efforts to get a job. Should the agency discover that a client has violated a rule, it may reduce or suspend payments. Our case study will focus on the attempt by a welfare agency to cut off payments to a recipient.

Through an investigation, the welfare agency has learned that Roger Ayde owns a home purchased, in better times, for five thousand dollars. He and his family still live in the house. However, according to Section 360 of the Social Service Law, a welfare beneficiary who owns a home can be required to give the agency a mortgage on it. The law gives discretion to the agency whether or not to enforce this regulation.

SOCIAL SERVICE LAW

360. Real property of legally responsible relatives; deeds and mortgages may be required.

1. The ownership of real property by an applicant or applicants, recipient or recipients who is or are legally responsible relatives of the child or children for whose benefit the application is made or the aid is granted, whether such ownership be individual or joint as tenants in common, tenants by the entirety

or joint tenants, shall not preclude the granting of aid to dependent children or the continuance thereof if he or they are without the necessary funds to maintain himself or themselves and such child or children. The social-services official may, however, require, as a condition to the granting of aid or the continuance thereof, that he be given a deed of or a mortgage on such property.

To carry out this responsibility, the agency drafted a rule of its own, elaborating on the original statute. Paragraph (a) summarizes the provisions of the Social Service Law. In paragraphs (b) and (c), the agency spells out the relevant considerations that will be taken into account in determining whether or not a mortgage shall be required for personal (non-income-producing) and rental (income-producing) property.

352.27 Real Property. (a) Ownership of real property by the applicant or recipient, or the spouse of such applicant or recipient in Aid to Aged, Blind and Disabled (AABD) or by the parent of a dependent child in Aid to Dependent Children (ADC), when such property is utilized as his home, shall not in and of itself make an individual ineligible for public assistance. A commissioner of social services may, however, in determining eligibility, take a deed, mortgage or lien on such property in accordance with sections 231.1(a) and 322 of the Social Service Law, taking into consideration the factors listed in subdivisions (b) and (c) of this section. He may take a deed or mortgage on the property of a parent of a child receiving ADC, in accordance with section 360 of the Social Service Law.

(b) A decision as to conservation, assignment or liquidation of non-income-producing property which is used as the client's home shall be based upon a consideration of the cost of carrying charges as compared with rental; marketability; the amount of client equity in the property; the client's age, health, and social situation, including the probable duration of dependency and the extent to which his social and economic rehabilitation or that of his dependent household are affected by conservation or liquidation of the property.

(c) A decision as to conservation, assignment or liquidation of income-producing property used as the client's home shall be based upon a consideration of the amount of assignable equity, probable duration of dependency, related social factors, the financial advantages of conserving income as compared with those of liquidation, and the costs of maintaining the property as compared with the amount of property income.

Having discovered that Ayde owned his own home, the agency demanded that he take out a mortgage, without informing him whether or not it took into account the various factors itemized in the agency regulation. Ayde refused, so the agency sent him a "Notice of Intent to Discontinue." The notice, actually a standard form, explains that Ayde will be denied further benefits because he has violated regulation 352.27; i.e. he has not taken out a mortgage on his house. In addition, the notice describes his right to a hearing.

	☐ Reduce	☒ Public Assistance
Notice of Intent to:		☐ Medical Assistance Authorization
	☒ Discontinue	☐ Food Stamp Authorization

To: ROGER AYDE	Case Number	999
	Category	ADC
	Date	9/4/75

This is to advise you that this department intends to:

☐ Reduce from _____ to _____ your Public Assistance Grant effective _____ .

☒ Discontinue your Public Assistance Grant on _____ 9/15/75.

☐ Reduce Coverage from _____ to _____

☒ Discontinue   Your Medical Assistance Authorization on 9/15/75.

☐ Reduce

Your Authorization to Purchase
Food Stamps on   9/15/75.

☒ Discontinue

for the following reason (s):

> You failed to comply with agency requirements by signing a
> mortgage on property you own (reg. 352.27).

It is important for you to note that even though the Medicaid Card
in your possession has an expiration date the end of the month, you
are not eligible to use this card beyond 9/15/75. Use of your
Medicaid Card beyond this date is illegal and prohibited.

You may have a conference at this department to review your case
at any time before the proposed date of the action noted above.

Susan Thompson	9/4/75
Signed	Date

Right to a Fair Hearing

If you believe that this action should not be taken, you may request
a state fair hearing by telephone or by writing to Fair Hearing Section. If you request a fair hearing, a notice will be sent to you informing you of the time and place of the hearing. At the hearing,
you, your attorney or other representative will have an opportunity
to present relevant written and oral evidence to demonstrate why
the action should not be taken as well as an opportunity to question
any persons who appear at the hearing and present evidence against
you. If you request a fair hearing before the date the action is proposed to be taken, you will continue to receive your assistance unchanged until the fair-hearing decision is issued. If you need help
in the fair hearing, contact one of the following community legal
services.

Ayde decides to request a hearing. Such decisions are
common, even if the individual does not have a good
reason, simply because the agency must continue to pro-

vide benefits until the hearing has concluded. In Ayde's case, though, he believes that the decision is unfair, and wishes to present his position. The agency sent him by regular mail a "Notice of Fair Hearing." Essentially, this document is like a summons in a court proceeding. It informs him of the place, date, and time of the hearing, advises him what materials to bring, and informs him of his rights. The form also specifies (paragraph 4) that he will continue to receive benefits until a decision is reached.

NOTICE OF FAIR HEARING

To: ROGER AYDE   (Appellant's name)

In response to your request for a fair hearing, your hearing will be held at the following time and place:

Place of Hearing: Executive Building   Date: 9/16/75
Time: 2:00 P.M.

INSTRUCTIONS TO PARTIES

1. You must bring to this hearing the following: this notice; witnesses, if any; all evidence that has a bearing on this case, including all books, records, and other forms of written evidence.

2. The appellant has the right to be represented by an attorney or other representative, to present documentary evidence, and to examine opposing witnesses and evidence.

3. The agency must provide for transportation for the appellant, his representatives and witnesses, and child-care and other costs related to attending the hearing, if necessary.

4. The agency SHALL/SHALL NOT continue the appellant's assistance, unchanged, until his fair-hearing decision is issued.

NOTICE TO APPELLANT

1. If you are not able to appear for your hearing at the time and place indicated above, please call telephone number   and explain why. Your grant of assistance will continue unchanged if you are not able to appear at that time and place for a good cause including any of the following: you are sick and unable to travel; you are not able to obtain a baby sitter; your attorney or representative is unable to appear. Failure to appear or to telephone will result in your assistance being discontinued.

2. If you no longer wish to have a fair hearing, please sign the statement below and return this notice.

I wish to withdraw my request for a fair hearing.

Signed: _____

Category and Case No. ADC 999
Agency: Representative:

Issue:
☒ Discontinuance   ☐ Suspension   ☐ Reduction
                    Date of Notice
                         9/9/75
☒ New
☐ Rescheduled

The next step is for the agency to explain why it wishes to discontinue Ayde's benefits. The document, prepared by the agency worker who made the decision, simply notes that payments have been discontinued because Ayde has not filed for a mortgage despite the agency's request that he do so. As with a complaint in a court, the summary defines the agency's claims and enables the recipient to prepare his case.

To: ROGER AYDE   Scheduled Hearing date: 9/16/75

                          Appellant: ROGER AYDE

                          Attorney or
                          Representative,   Legal Services
                          if any

FAIR HEARING SUMMARY

Case name, category and case number: Roger Ayde   ADC 999

Names, ages and relationship of persons affected:
   Roger Ayde   4/4/40
   5 minor children

Action which prompted request for Fair Hearing:

PA discontinuance

Brief description of facts, evidence and reasons supporting above action: (Include identification of specific provisions of law, Board Rules, Department Regulations and approved local policies which support decision):

The agency has requested as a condition for continuing appellant's public assistance, that he give the agency a mortgage on real property owned by him. Appellant has refused to do so; therefore, Social Service Law 360. Dept. Reg. 352.27.   (See attachments)

Relevant Budget or Budgets:	Special Grants:
Needs and Income Date	Period Covered — Item Amount

	Copy to:
Submitted by Susan Thompson Date: 9/16/75	☒ Appellant
	Representative ☐

Attach copy of Agency's written decision to appellant(s).

On September 16, 1975, as indicated in the Notice of Fair Hearing, the adjudication began. A hearing officer assigned by the agency conducts matters. The agency representative argues for the agency, while Roger Ayde is represented by a worker from a local legal-assistance project. First, the agency representative gives a short opening statement and introduces a letter from the County Clerk's Office stating that Ayde does indeed own the property in question (in a court of law, this document would probably be inadmissible since it is not direct testimony by anyone). The agency worker testifies that she asked Ayde to sign a mortgage but he refused. Then, she said, she informed him that benefits would be discontinued due to his refusal, and had the Notice of Intent to Discontinue sent out.

Ayde's representative cross-examines the agency worker.

She admits that she did not check the elements mentioned in the regulation. In particular, she did not look into the salability of the property, the likely duration of Ayde's need for public assistance, or the effects of the mortgage on Ayde's financial situation when he got off welfare. The cross-examination ended, and the agency rested its case.

In his opening statement, Ayde's representative stressed the fact that the agency had violated its own rule regarding factors to be considered before demanding a mortgage. He presented an "affidavit" (written statement made under oath) stating that, in the present housing market, Ayde's home is not salable at a reasonable price. Next, the representative had Ayde testify. Ayde reported that he had been on welfare for just five months and expected to go off it soon, since he had needed it only because of an illness from which he had now recovered. He also testified that his home needed repairs; he therefore needed to execute a mortgage to finance the reconstruction. However, no financial institution will advance him any money if there is already a welfare mortgage on the house. In fact, Ayde said, a welfare mortgage would disrupt his entire economic status, already burdened with a number of large unpaid debts.

On cross-examination Ayde admitted that he had no outstanding job prospects. He was asked to describe the repairs his home needed. In response, he mentioned a leaky roof, an inadequate electric system, and crumbling masonry. The cross-examination ended, and Ayde's representative rested his case. Both sides waived closing argument.

After the hearing concluded, the hearing officer reviewed the evidence and wrote an initial decision, finding in Ayde's favor. The decision begins by describing the nature of the case.

In the Matter of Appeal of :
      ROGER AYDE   DECISION AFTER
from a determination by the   :   FAIR HEARING
Department of Social Services
(hereinafter called the agency)   :

A fair hearing was held at Executive Building, on September 16, 1975, before John Hall, Hearing Officer, at which the appellant, the appellant's representative and representatives of the agency appeared. The appeal is from a determination by the agency relating to proposed discontinuance of a grant of aid to dependent children. An opportunity to be heard having been accorded all interested parties and the evidence having been taken and due deliberation having been had, it is hereby found:

The next three paragraphs review the events that led up to the hearing.

(1) The appellant and his five minor children are currently in receipt of a recurring cash grant of aid to dependent children. The appellant is the owner of the home in which the family resides.

(2) On July 24, 1975, the agency sent the appellant a written request, requiring him to sign a mortgage in favor of the agency, against his property, as a condition to the family's continued eligibility for aid to dependent children.

(3) The agency sent a Notice of Intent to Discontinue appellant's grant on September 4, 1975, to be effective September 15, 1975. The appellant requested a fair hearing to review the agency's proposed action on September 5, 1975. The agency was notified that appellant's grant must be continued without change until a fair-hearing decision is issued. The agency has continued assistance unchanged to the appellant through the date of this hearing, and the agency has stated that assistance will be continued until a fair-hearing decision is issued.

Paragraphs (4) and (5) are crucial. In paragraph (4), the decision summarizes the regulation and notes the requirement for an investigation before a mortgage is demanded. Paragraph (5) finds that no such investigation took place.

(4) The appellant advised the agency that he refused to comply with the request to execute a mortgage against his property.

Subdivision (a) of Section 352.27 of the Regulations of the State Department of Social Services provides that a social-services official may, in determining continuing eligibility for public assistance, require such recipients owning an interest in real property to execute a deed, mortgage or lien on such property. However, said regulation also requires that the agency undertake the investigation set out in 352.27(b).

(5) The agency undertook no investigation of the marketability of the home, the likely duration of appellant's need for public assistance, or the effect of the mortgage on appellant once off public assistance.

Paragraph (6) is of particular interest. Theoretically, once the hearing officer had determined that proper procedure had not been followed and that the agency had no good reason for failing to do so, he should rule immediately for Ayde. Realistically, though, the hearing officer wants to point out that such an investigation would have made a difference. There were factors in Ayde's situation that make a mortgage inadvisable. He therefore records those items.

(6) The appellant's home is not presently marketable. Appellant has been on assistance only a short time and may soon return to full-time employment. Appellant's home is in need of repairs that can only be financed by a mortgage on said home.

Next, the decision makes its legal findings. Clearly, Section 352.27 of the regulations is applicable. Thus, under certain circumstances Ayde could be compelled to take out a mortgage or lose further benefits. The regulation, however, also requires an investigation, and this the agency failed to carry out. Consequently, the agency cannot cut off payments to Ayde. The decision overrules the agency's actions.

The record in this case establishes that appellant is the owner of the home in which the family resides. The agency has requested a mortgage against such property as a condition for the appellant's continued eligibility for aid to dependent children. The record establishes that the agency failed to carry out the investigation required by 352.27(b). At this fair hearing the agency did not establish sufficient reason for its failure to comply with the regulations. Accordingly, the agency's determination proposing to discontinue appellant's grant is incorrect.

DECISION: The determination of the agency is not and cannot be affirmed. The agency is directed to take appropriate action in accordance with the foregoing decision pursuant to the provisions of Section 352.27 of the regulations.

The hearing officer sends his initial decision and a copy of the record of the case to the head of the welfare agency, who passes it on to the official in charge of such matters, the assistant counsel for hearing decisions. After reviewing the case, the assistant counsel confirms the hearing officer's determination. The decision is then typed and sent to Ayde, as well as to the agency. Had Ayde lost, he would have had the right to take the matter to court.

Procedurally, this adjudicatory hearing more closely resembles a courtroom proceeding than the legislative process, although the rules for administrative agencies are not as strict as those which are used by the courts. The impact of the decision, though, is much more restricted (at least than a civil case). The decision contains no rationale that might later be applied in other, similar cases. Unlike a court opinion or a statute, then, an administrative ruling affects only the party directly involved. Given the emphasis on speed over deliberation in administration hearings, this limited impact is undoubtedly for the best.

In our society, laws are created by a wide variety of people and institutions. Individuals, companies, agencies, legislatures, and courts are all part of the lawmaking process. This proliferation of lawmakers can easily make for confusion. In truth, ours is a legalistic country, perhaps too much so for our own good. Yet, with our complex structures and manifold problems, it is hard to see just which lawmakers we could usefully dispense with. Contracts, courts, legislatures, agencies—each deals with a different aspect of our lives, each has its own special features, and none could easily replace any of the others. As long as we continue to believe in a "government of laws, not of men," we shall also continue to rely, occasionally excessively, on our lawmaking institutions.

9

The People
and the Law

During the Renaissance, people used to compare laws to a
spider's web—closely spun to catch the smallest gnat, but
too weak to hold back the rats. There was, and is, much
truth in this observation. Indisputably, in many cases law
serves the interests of special powerful groups and not the
people as a whole. Tax shelters, subsidies, differential criminal conviction rates (poor people are more often found
guilty of crimes than the rich), all exemplify the biases
that often show themselves in the law.

But the evidence is not that one-sided. Just as there are
clear instances of small groups dominating the law, so,
too, are there cases in which the public interest has
triumphed. Individual citizens have successfully bucked
city hall, the rights of the poor have been vindicated, and
every once in a while the government actually does something right. We would all be more impressed by these
facts were it not that, after all, law is supposed always to
promote the general welfare and serve no particular individual or group. That this does not occur forces us to ex-

amine more closely the relations between the public and the law.

Law is not made in a vacuum. While doing their jobs, lawmakers encounter a wide variety of pressure groups seeking to realize their vision of the common good or to further their special interests, or both. The results of pressure tactics are hard to estimate, but groups that use them frequently do achieve their objectives. Whether one judges this process to be good or bad depends on how one feels about the goals involved. Lobbying itself is inevitable and, indeed, inherent in the democratic process.

People trying to influence the law use four distinct tactics. First, the group can attempt to build popular support for its aims, usually by propaganda or publicity campaigns. A full-fledged assault calls for getting the public's attention, associating the proposed idea with some beliefs or institutions that are already popular, and then stimulating the people to support the policy. Successful propaganda campaigns of this sort are costly and difficult to organize. However, as the importance of mass communications continues to grow, more and more groups are making the effort.

The other pressure techniques rely on affecting the behavior of lawmakers directly, not via public pressure. The simplest way for groups to gain their ends is to install friendly officials in key posts, whether elected or appointed. Along these lines, groups may participate in elections or press those who make appointments to choose sympathetic nominees. If this device fails, the group may contact the lawmakers themselves and try to persuade them to adopt the group's viewpoint, either by personal discussions or through letters. The fourth method frequently used by political groups is providing information to lawmakers. When a group can supply accurate and persuasive material, they can often win someone over to their position.

Because there exists such a variety of lawmakers, pressure groups do not need to restrict their work to a single branch of government. A defeat in one arena may be reversed by a victory in another (and vice versa). To understand lobbies, therefore, we must look at the various lawmakers once again.

People and the Legislatures

Legislatures have been the focus of pressure groups since the United States was founded; in fact, the word "lobbying" comes from political activity in legislative halls. The fragmentation of power in legislatures makes them especially open to external pressures. Once a friendly legislator has been identified, a group can concentrate its efforts on working with that individual to further their common aims. This relationship, of course, is also advantageous to the legislator in terms of political support and information.

As we have seen, the committee system prevails in most legislatures. The existence of these small, specialized bodies makes the task of the legislative lobbyist considerably easier than it would be otherwise. First, it enables pressure groups to concentrate their attention on the few people who are responsible on a continuing basis for recommending laws in their field of interest. The support of the relevant committee is usually, though not always, tantamount to success. Second, the utilization of public and private hearings by committees offers groups a legitimate forum for the expression of their views; indeed, this opportunity for exposure is one of the main purposes of legislative hearings. The existence of several, often competing, committees, finally, provides a means for a pressure group, intent on blocking a proposal, to do so. In general, given the fragmentation of power in legislatures and their tendency to compromise, groups trying to preserve the status quo have a basic advantage over those seeking change. Reform groups find this situation constantly frustrating.

All four of the basic pressure-group tactics are applicable to legislatures: publicity campaigns, election activity, persuasion, and fact gathering. The last technique is probably the most effective. Legislators are not normally incompetent or corrupt. They want to do what is best for their country and their constituents, partly out of a sense of duty, partly to get re-elected. However, they rarely have at their disposal staffs capable of answering detailed questions about technical aspects of proposed legislation. Here is where the pressure group enters the picture. By providing data and analysis, the group can attempt to show the lawmaker that their proposal is in truth in the public interest and so ought to be supported. Lobbyists have thus become an essential part of the legislative process.

Despite the value of lobbyists, legislators recognize that they can also represent a threat to the democratic system, and legislatures have devised ways of controlling them. Most effective in the short run is investigation of the overzealous. Rarely does a year go by that somewhere in the United States a lobbyist is not accused of improper activities, ranging from illegal campaign contributions to outright bribery. Of more long-lasting effect are rules requiring lobbyists to register, identify their employers, and declare the sources and extent of their finances. This information is usually made public in the expectation that unethical behavior will be discouraged. In addition, of course, certain types of "lobbying," such as buying votes, have been banned altogether.

These restrictions, however, should not distract attention from the basic point. With few exceptions, American legislatures regard lobbying as an entirely legitimate aspect of democratic politics. To be sure, they provide political aid to individual lawmakers and occasionally overstep their proper bounds. Their main function, though, is to present the ideas and opinions of a body of citizens who want to see their views embodied in the law. As such, lobbying is a form of "the right of the people peaceably to assemble,

and to petition the Government for a redress of grievances," guaranteed by the First Amendment to the Constitution.

People and the Administrative Agencies

Pressure groups may be important in legislatures, but their
impact is minimal compared to their influence on agencies. Since agencies carry out specialized functions, each
agency usually focuses on a single area of concern and regulates groups performing similar jobs. This type of specialization ensures that the people being regulated will organize together in a pressure group to deal with the
agency. It is comparable to collective bargaining. Since the
groups share their relationship with the agency, they can
easily recognize the advantages of a united front. Their
continued interaction with their regulators gives them co-
hesion.

This interaction is equally vital to the agency. For the
agency to do its job, it must reach an understanding with
the groups it regulates. The agency cannot be everywhere
at once, supervising every action. It must have the voluntary co-operation of its clientele if it is to function. Naturally, this co-operation has a price: a say in agency policies.
As we have seen, the entire rule-making procedure of administrative agencies is designed to give groups an opportunity to present their views before the rules go into effect.

The relationship between outside groups and agencies
differs in significant ways from the legislature-lobby interaction. For instance, agencies have experts of their own
to gather and interpret information. Unlike legislators,
then, administrators do not rely heavily on lobbyists for
data or facts. Such material is gathered from groups informally and during hearings, but its impact is relatively
small. Instead, agencies and groups co-operate in identifying problems and disputed issues for resolution.

Yet the role of pressure groups in the selection of administrators is far greater than their influence on the electoral process. A stockbroker or securities lawyer is no more likely than anyone else to be elected to Congress. However, when it comes to choosing a member of the Securities and Exchange Commission, which regulates stocks, the situation is different. A regulator has to know how the regulated groups operate in order to supervise them properly, and few people understand an organization better than its members. Thus, one finds transportation executives on transportation regulatory boards, farmers on farm agencies, and nuclear physicists making the rules for nuclear power plants. The potential channels for influence are clear.

Similarly, a member of an administrative agency whose term has expired, or who is looking for another job, is most likely to find employment in the very field he has been regulating. Agency officials inevitably, in the course of their duties, acquire considerable expertise in the area their agency works. Naturally enough, private groups wish to make use of this expertise when it offers itself on the open market. This phenomenon also appears in legislatures (former legislators often become professional lobbyists), but it runs rampant in agencies. The result is an almost incestuous relationship between the rule makers and the rule obeyers.

Pressure groups can increase their influence by participating in the agency funding process. As we have noted, most agencies need periodic appropriations from a legislature to survive, and pressure groups can easily switch their attention to this arena. Lobbyists rarely try to discipline agencies by working to have their funds reduced. On the contrary, the working partnership between agencies and pressure groups is so close that the two join together to keep the agency going. Without the political support of those being regulated, most agencies would find it difficult to obtain the money they need.

There is another major difference between legislative

and administrative lobbying. With legislatures, the average citizen has as much chance to be heard as a high-powered organization (or almost as much). True, the well-financed pressure group can hire professional lobbyists to present their point of view. Legislators, however, realize that these people are being paid to say what they do, and discount their remarks accordingly. Unless the group has voting power in back of it, its influence will be determined largely by the reliability of the information it provides and the persuasiveness of its arguments.

The story is different with individuals. Legislators suspect that anyone concerned enough to write a letter or to try to contact a congressman or an assemblyman personally is probably concerned enough to work at the next election for or against a candidate, and can probably influence others to do the same. Except for obvious crank letters, most communications to legislators are taken very seriously indeed. Form letters may be discounted, but few ignore home-town sentiment altogether, and those few are rarely re-elected. In their own way, then, the people can have an impact on their government, if they choose to exert the effort.

Administrative agencies, though, do not operate this way. In the first place, agency officials are not usually elected. Still more significantly, the matters they deal with are normally so technical and specialized that the average citizen probably cannot even understand the problem, much less propose a solution. Public opinion is easily dismissed by agency experts as "emotional and uninformed," not to be taken into account except as a nuisance. In dealing with agencies, pressure groups have all the cards.

Finally, few effective controls exist to regulate administrative lobbying. Bribery, of course, is illegal, but little else is prohibited. The combined impact of all these factors has been to transform agencies into the representatives not of the people but of the groups they were established to regulate. Agencies have been captured by their subjects. They have come to view themselves as protectors of groups, and they see their duty as minimizing pressure on those being regulated. Obviously, there is a need for better controls over administrative-agency behavior. The existing alliance between the regulators and the regulated simply fails to serve the public interest.

People and the Courts

Of all the lawmaking bodies, courts appear on the surface to be freest of external pressures. Personal lobbying is virtually impossible. The administrative-agency maneuver of offering a judge a position when he leaves the court is illegal and useless, since most judges have no intention of retiring. Pressure groups can affect the appointment of judges, to be sure, but since most federal and many state judges are chosen for life, there is little a group can do if the judge does not live up (or down) to their expectations. Even where judges are elected, it is considered unethical to campaign against a candidate on policy grounds. The judicial system, in fact, was constructed to shield the courts from outside forces and permit them to act in impartial solitude.

Lawyers are also restricted in their activities. Certainly, bar associations have not been shy about making policy recommendations, but there are limits set by the Code of Professional Responsibility on some types of advocacy. For instance, attorneys are forbidden to engage in "barratry"; that is, they cannot go around stirring up litigation. Similarly, "champerty," which is taking over someone else's legal rights for purposes of a lawsuit (thus, a firm might find people who cannot afford to sue, even though they have strong cases, and buy them out, so that the firm could sue and keep the winnings), is also prohibited. Equally unacceptable is "solicitation," i.e. seeking out clients, or "ambulance-chasing" (although, as we mentioned in Chapter 3, this rule has been modified recently). All these rules curtail the influence of pressure groups and attorneys.

From another perspective, though, the courts depend more on pressure groups than any other institution in the United States. For, unlike legislatures and administrative agencies, courts cannot investigate problems on their own. Someone must bring a case to them before they can take action. In this sense, the judiciary is the most passive branch of government, the most vulnerable lawmaker.

Thus, individual citizens with time and money can genuinely affect the court process. Some of the most important and influential court cases in history were brought by ordinary people concerned to vindicate their rights. For example, the Supreme Court ruled that anyone accused of a major crime had the right to an attorney, as the result of a handwritten petition presented by a convicted felon (*Gideon* v. *Wainwright*). Cases holding official Bible readings in public schools unconstitutional, upholding tax exemption for churches, nullifying some of Roosevelt's New Deal, and fixing the limits on pornography, were all brought by private persons. In principle, and to a large extent in practice, courts are open to everyone.

Nevertheless, pressure groups have not abandoned the judicial field. The judicial process does offer advantages to interest-group litigation. Groups can bring cases that present their cause in the most favorable light. Over a long term, they can bring a series of cases to build up their position gradually. Often, they can choose which court (state or federal) will hear their cases and so improve their prospects for victory. Group-inspired law has played an increasingly large role in the judicial system.

There are a number of legal techniques pressure groups can use in their judicial activities. Perhaps the most basic is the "test case." On the face of it, a test case is an ordinary suit challenging some law or procedure. However, in reality such litigation is not concerned so much with the individual plaintiff as with the over-all validity of the act in question and its effect on the entire group. The school-desegregation suits, for instance, were originally brought by just one student or family, but they actually represented the grievances of a much larger group of people. Their case symbolized a broader controversy.

Similar in purpose, though differing in approach, is the "class action." The principle behind the class-action suit is that a few people bring a suit representing the total number of persons actually involved. If many people, for example, have been harmed by the actions of a corporation, but none of them have suffered a serious enough injury to make a challenge financially worthwhile, they can, in effect, combine their efforts into a single lawsuit. However, there is a catch to the class action. Once a claim has been filed and the case decided, no other member of the original class represented in the suit may again go to court on the issue. This holds true even if someone was one of the injured people, and therefore a member of the class, but did not even know the suit was being brought.

Despite this drawback, which seems unfair on its face but which is probably necessary to prevent endless litigation, the class action can be of great value to groups. For example, one of the largest of such suits was brought in 1968, when about forty-two thousand people were represented in a case against pharmaceutical companies producing the drug tetracycline. The plaintiffs claimed that the price of the drug had been artificially raised (price fixing). The settlement out of court, reached in 1970, led to the distribution of one hundred million dollars to the victims of the overpricing. (Not all the purchasers could be found, so the federal court directed that any remainder from the settlement be given to state governments to be held in trust "for the benefit of consumers generally.")

Even after a case has been launched, it is still possible for groups to involve themselves. The best known method for doing so is the *"amicus curiae"* brief. Literally, *amicus curiae* means "friend of the court," and an *amicus* brief is indeed an act of friendship. When an issue comes before a court, and an outside party "has a concrete, substantial interest in the decision of the case," it may submit an *amicus* brief. This device is used with especial skill by ideological organizations with permanent legal staffs, e.g. the American Civil Liberties Union, the Environmental Defense Fund, and so on.

The groups, of course, seize on the opportunity of an *amicus* brief to present their case to the judge, particularly if their arguments and views differ in some ways from the actual litigants'. From the court's point of view, the advantage of *amicus* briefs is that they may present new ideas and information not brought out by the parties. Pressure groups that specialize in *amicus* briefs have usually acquired considerable expertise in their field of interest, and their briefs are often more illuminating than any others. Yet courts will reject or ignore briefs that are simply blatant attempts to pressure the judges. Incidentally, even without preparing an *amicus* brief, a pressure group can provide substantial help to litigants with whom it sympathizes. A group may decide it is more profitable to help someone else with a brief than to write one of their own.

Pressure groups can also co-ordinate their activities on a long-range basis. They may hold training and planning conferences to exchange information with other, likeminded practitioners. Sometimes they will encourage the preparation of articles for law reviews or other journals, an important influence on judges. In a few instances, groups may plan a whole series of cases, each designed to bring the law a little closer to where they finally want it. How widespread such activity is remains unclear, but there have been a few striking records of success (Jehovah's Witnesses, the National Association for the Advancement of Colored People).

There are other ways to lobby the judiciary. Very important is one we just mentioned: law reviews. Law reviews are journals, usually quarterlies, published at law schools by the students. They review legal developments and propose new ideas and concepts. Since the use of these journals by judges and their clerks is substantial, groups publishing articles favorable to their point of view may exert some influence, especially if the authors are respected and well known in the field and the journals prestigious. Nor are courts oblivious to political pressures. Much as they try to be impartial, judges cannot help but be influenced by the events around them. There are many examples, especially but not exclusively in lower courts, of judges following the election returns.

The ultimate way to affect a court is to change the law. Even constitutional interpretation by the Supreme Court can be overruled by an amendment, requiring a vote by two thirds of the Congress and three fourths of the states. Cumbersome as the amending process is, it has been used three or four times for exactly this purpose. The Sixteenth Amendment, for instance, establishing the income tax, was passed after the Supreme Court had ruled an earlier tax bill unconstitutional. Court decisions based on statutory interpretation, certainly, are more easily reversed. The legislature simply rewrites the statute.

Finally, we must remember that just because a court announces a decision, this does not mean it is followed. Courts have no troops or police at their disposal. When force is required to apply a decision, the judiciary must turn to other branches of government for assistance. Even ignoring cases of forcible resistance or civil disobedience, there will still be situations in which judicial rulings will be disregarded. A town justice in northwestern Missouri was paid a fee by his town only when he found a defendant guilty. When informed that the Supreme Court had declared the practice unconstitutional (for obvious reasons), he replied, "I didn't know the Supreme Court had jurisdiction up here."

Legal Frontiers

The scope of law in our society grows steadily. Federal courts handled 60,000 cases in 1960; the figure for 1975 was 150,000. New problems arise, new social relationships develop, new litigants find their way into court, and the law expands. We cannot mention all the new directions the law is taking, or predict the results that will be achieved, but we can point out a few of the issues currently agitating the legal system.

One matter of great interest at present is the environment. The United States, the land of plenty, is not as plentiful as it once was. Natural resources are being consumed much too rapidly, and the resultant waste products litter and pollute our lives. Since the late 1950s, people have become more aware of the problems we may be facing soon. Inevitably, they have turned to the law as the one social institution capable of regulating the consumption and halting the disaster before it becomes irreversible.

The legal response to the environmental issue exhibits many of the features of law that we have discussed. Congress has passed legislation, for example the National Environmental Policy Act of 1969. The Environmental Protection Agency has been created to administer our resources. Simultaneously, pressure groups have entered the fray: the Environmental Defense Fund, working in the courts; the Sierra Club, which works on legislatures; and many others. Propaganda campaigns have been organized both by environmentalists and by their opponents. Not all the activity has been useful, or even consistent, but the law has certainly responded to the crisis, one way or another.

A second region of legal advance has been the right of privacy. Back in 1890, future Supreme Court Justice Louis Brandeis collaborated on an article, published in the *Harvard Law Review*, titled "The Right to Privacy." Only in the past few decades, however, have the lawmaking bodies of our country truly begun to grapple with the implications of this right. Part of the new interest resulted from the impact of modern technology. When modern bugging and eavesdropping devices were invented, people soon realized the threat they raised to individual rights, and the fight was on. This particular aspect of the right to privacy is one of the most confused, legally speaking. At one point, the Supreme Court ruled that microphones hammered through a wall violated constitutional protections against illegal entry into one's home; microphones that could be used from outside the house, though, were permissible. Both courts and legislatures have moved on to more sophisticated treatments of the problem, but problem it has stayed.

The impact of modern technology on privacy need not have sinister motives behind it. The expanded use of citizens' band radios, innocent devices in and of themselves, has brought with it some intriguing new problems. Not only do CB users interfere with each other's transmissions, they sometimes infringe on the privacy of non-users, who begin to hear strange conversations coming over their television sets or out of their microwave ovens. How can the rights of non-users be protected without restricting the rights of users to communicate freely over public airways? Here is a problem that the law must tackle.

The right to privacy has other aspects, all well publicized. For instance, there is the supposed right to sexual preferences: the right to be a homosexual without suffering discrimination for that reason. Thus far, most courts have not accepted this claim, but some local legislatures have begun to revise their statutes to take this new demand into account. And, of course, homosexuals have started organizing into pressure groups.

The issue of abortion, also connected to the right of privacy by its supporters (the sanctity of the doctor-patient relationship), is not a new one, but it is particularly lively at the present time. Topical also is the "right to die" question. Medical technology is now capable, at tremendous expense, of prolonging life almost indefinitely in those who would otherwise pass on. Does a person, or the person's family, have the right to refuse further treatment and let the patient die? A lower New Jersey court said no (the state's Supreme Court reversed), a California legislature says yes. It will be some time before this matter is resolved.

Let's give one more example, this time from the seemingly dull field of commercial law. According to a traditional doctrine called "holder in due course," a lender is not responsible for the performance, delivery, or quality of goods and service for which the borrower has contracted. We have previously discussed a car purchase; in that example, the buyer borrowed money from a financial institution to pay for the automobile. Under the holder-in-due-course theory, if the car did not work, that was the buyer's problem, not the lender's. The buyer had to continue making payments to the lender, while pursuing action against the original dealer.

This policy dates back to a time when financial institutions lent mainly to capitalist entrepreneurs, not private consumers. As far as the quality of purchased goods was concerned, these businessmen could take care of themselves. Their need was money. If a bank had to take the responsibility for the goods being purchased, it would be more reluctant to lend the capital, and the entrepreneur would suffer. The doctrine of holder in due course protected the lender, thus making money available for business expansion.

In our day, the situation has changed. The development of installment buying and credit cards has made borrowing a common practice among ordinary people, not just big businesses. For such individuals, consumer protection is more important than availability of capital. The holder-in-due-course theory, however, provides no protection to the consumer.

Indeed, the law was actually used to carry out various swindles. For instance, a shady dealer might sell television sets at very low prices and easy credit terms to unsuspecting customers. Financing would be handled by an equally shady lending agency. The dealer would then skip town, and when the shoddy sets broke down, the purchasers would be stuck. Since the lending agency was now the holder in due course, it was not responsible for the quality of the televisions, and the customers had to continue making payments. To be sure, they could sue the dealer, but only if they could find him. The lending agency and the dealer, meanwhile, would split the profits.

To prevent such swindles, the law had to be adjusted to modern conditions. Therefore, as of 1976 the Federal Trade Commission (a national administrative agency) ruled that a consumer may legally withhold payment from a creditor—the holder in due course—if the merchandise was defective. The lender must then sue the original seller, not the purchaser, to recover his money. In other words, the holder in due course no longer enjoys immunity while the buyer suffers.

The impact of such a policy change may be profound. In practice, it is quite difficult to persuade manufacturers and dealers to respond significantly to individual complaints. They support product quality in principle, but it is difficult for them to deal with single cases even if they want to. With the weight of banks and loan companies added in on the side of the consumer, however, we may expect to see some action.

This list could be extended indefinitely. In every instance, though, the same basic points would appear. Always, the law responds in various ways to new demands made upon it. Various legal institutions take various approaches, see matters from various perspectives, arrive at various conclusions. Always, the law changes as conditions in the society change, as our needs change, as our ideals change. And always, law tries but fails to embody within itself the final resolution of our disputes and problems. The law is inescapably imperfect. It must be so, because it is we, ultimately, who make it.

A Guide
to Further Reading

Those interested in pursuing the nature of law would do well to begin with Lon Fuller's short *Anatomy of the Law* (New York, 1968). Fun, if accessible in a local law library, is his science-fiction piece on law "The Case of the Speluncean Explorers," 62 *Harvard Law Review* 616 (1949)—the legal form for citing Volume 62, page 616. More detail is available in Carl Friedrich's medium-sized survey *Philosophy of Law in Historical Perspective* (Chicago, 1963) and still more in Wolfgang Friedman's *Legal Theory* (New York, 1967). A better way to get an idea of the meaning of law is to read what legal theorists have said about it in their own words. Although many books of legal theory are long and dryly technical, there are a few short and readable ones: Benjamin Cardozo, *Nature of the Judicial Process* (New Haven, 1921) and *The Growth of the Law* (New Haven, 1924); H. L. A. Hart, *Concept of the Law* (New York, 1961); Edward Levi, *An Introduction to Legal Reasoning* (Chicago, 1962); and any of a number of works by Roscoe Pound, for example *Social*

Control Through Law (New Haven, 1942). The quotation from Oliver Wendell Holmes in Chapter 1 comes from his often anthologized article "The Path of the Law," 10 *Harvard Law Review* 457 (1897).

Samuel Mermin's short paperback *Law and the Legal System* (Boston, 1973) provides a good review of the functions of law. For an anthology treating law in other societies, there is Laura Nader, Ed., *Law in Culture and Society* (Chicago, 1969). C. Gordon Post's *Introduction to Law* (Englewood Cliffs, N.J., 1963) focuses on the history of law. For a fuller analysis of the types of law, one will probably have to try a law-school textbook, perhaps William Schantz, *The American Legal Environment* (St. Paul, 1976). The study by Karl Llewellyn *The Common Law Tradition* (Boston, 1960), referred to in Chapter 2, is very good but rather advanced for the beginner.

Henry Abraham's *The Judicial Process* (New York, 1975) is a fine introduction to the judiciary in general. The literature on the Supreme Court is enormous. A good place to start is Alexander Bickel, *The Least Dangerous Branch* (Indianapolis, 1962). For the historical background, there is a very readable survey by Leo Pfeffer, *This Honorable Court* (Boston, 1965). Another way to study the Supreme Court is to watch it in action, for instance in Anthony Lewis' little classic *Gideon's Trumpet* (New York, 1964), which covers the case of *Gideon* v. *Wainwright*. For a more up-to-date report, see Warren Weaver's article in the New York *Times* "The Supreme Court at Work," February 6, 1975.

Herbert Jacobs presents a full, if unexciting, review of the American court system in *Justice in America* (Boston, 1972). Charles Ashman presents another perspective in *The Finest Judges Money Can Buy* (Los Angeles, 1973). Meanwhile, Roscoe Pound's old critique of the court system still retains its vitality: "The Causes of Popular Dissatisfaction with the Administration of Justice," 29 *American Bar Association Reports*, Part I, 395 (1906).

The standard history of legal education in the United States is *Legal Education in the United States*, by Albert Harno (San Francisco, 1953). As an introductory book, though, we recommend John Dobbyn's *So You Want to Go to Law School* (St. Paul, 1976), a short, well-written paperback that goes well beyond its title. Anyone seriously interested in going to law school must consult the *Pre-Law Handbook*, published annually by the Association of American Law Schools, the Law School Admission Council, and the Educational Testing Service. This volume discusses pre-law training, law as a career, and, most important, each law school in the United States accredited by the American Bar Association. Karl Llewellyn's old lectures, published as *The Bramble Bush* (Dobbs Ferry, N.Y., 1960), provide a good account of the case-study method. Occasionally a publisher will come out with a book explaining how a person can do his own legal work and save lots of money. Our advice is to put such tomes on the bookshelves next to *Lord of the Rings* and other fantasies. Except in Small Claims Court, even lawyers hire other lawyers. There is an old legal saying: "An attorney who represents himself has a fool for a client." That goes double for the lay public.

The legal profession is surveyed by Martin Mayer in *The Lawyers* (New York, 1967) and, in a more scholarly way, by Vern Countryman and Ted Finman, *The Lawyer in Modern Society* (Boston, 1966). Both books are quite long. Readers looking for a lighter approach can try the writings of lawyer-novelist Louis Auchincloss, for example *Powers of Attorney* (Boston, 1963). More critical examinations are provided by Ralph Nader and Mark Green, Eds., *Verdicts on Lawyers* (New York, 1976), and from a historical point of view, Jerold Auerbach, *Unequal Justice* (New York, 1976).

For further information on contract law, the reader will have to locate a law-school textbook; there are no good popular treatments. Anyone with car problems, however, could profitably consult Ralph Nader, Lowell Dodge, and Ralf Hotchkiss, *What to Do with Your Bad Car* (New York, 1971). Our analysis of contracts of adhesion is based on the case of *Henningsen* v. *Bloomfield Motors, Inc.*, 32 N.J. 358 (Supreme Court of New Jersey, 1960).

The best books on legislatures deal with the U. S. Congress. As an overview, we recommend David Mayhew, *Congress: the Electoral Connection* (New Haven, 1974), supplemented perhaps with Robert Peabody's study of the passage of a campaign finance bill, *To Enact a Law* (New York, 1972), or one of the many other, similar volumes. Books on state legislatures tend to fall into the category of college textbooks, such as William Keefe and Morris Ogul, *American Legislative Process* (Englewood Cliffs, N.J., 1968). Our case is derived from two real cases: *Belle Terre* v. *Boraas* 416 U.S. 1 (1974) and *Plains* v. *Ferraioli*, 34 N.Y. 2d 300 (New York Court of Appeals, 1974). (We shall explain how to read these citations in a moment.)

Again, the best source for material on the judicial process, other than the books we have already mentioned, is a law school textbook. We ourselves made use of the still unpublished work by Henry Hart and Albert Sacks, *The Legal Process*. The criminal-justice system, on the other hand, has attracted a wealth of contributors. For some contrasting views, there are Ramsey Clark, *Crime in America* (New York, 1970); Ernest van den Haag, *Punishing Criminals* (New York, 1975); James Wilson, *Thinking About Crime* (New York, 1975). There are also two books of special interest: Harry Kalven and Hans Zeisel, *The American Jury* (Boston, 1966), and Ronald Goldfarb, *Jails* (New York, 1975). Patrick Murphy's *Our Kindly Parent, the State* (New York, 1974) will serve as an introduction to the problems of juvenile justice. Our rental case, and the theory of the implied warrant of habitability, come from *Javins* v. *First National Realty Corp.*, 428 F. 2nd 1071 (Washington, D.C., Circuit, 1970).

Administrative law is a field of its own in law schools, with its own textbooks, which are unhelpful for the average citizen. For a background to regulatory commissions, the basic work is by Marver Bernstein and is called *Regulating Business by Independent Commission* (Princeton, N.J., 1955). Ralph Nader's associates have produced a series of more up-to-date and readable, if somewhat over-critical, studies of various administrative agencies, starting with the Federal Trade Commission. Our welfare client is based on a real individual who encountered this problem in New York State; we have borrowed that state's legal forms. The underlying law comes from *Goldberg* v. *Kelly*, 397 *U.S.* 254 (1970).

The classic study of pressure groups in the United States is David Truman's *Governmental Process* (New York, 1971). It is complete, long, and not light reading. Probably it would be easier to look over analyses of pressure groups in action, such as Thomas Murphy, *Pressures upon Congress* (Woodbury, N.Y., 1973), or Grant McConnell, *Private Power and American Democracy* (New York, 1966). Frank Sorauf has written an especially good book on pressure groups and the judicial process: *The Wall of Separation* (Princeton, N.J., 1976). For a more skeptical view of the influence of groups in court, compare Nathan Hakman, "Lobbying the Supreme Court," 35 *Fordham Law Review* 15.

People, of course, do not write books about future laws. Most of the developments we mentioned in our last chapter are too recent to be in book form yet. One general article worth looking at is by Thomas Erlich, "Legal Pollution," in the New York *Times Magazine* of February 8, 1976. However, anyone who wants to investigate current problems must be prepared to do legal research on his own.

There is an incredible volume of publications on American law, reaching the point that no single library, except perhaps the Library of Congress, possesses anything close to a complete set of legal literature. Instead, each law firm

and most governmental units, especially counties, usually
have their own law libraries, containing a selection of the
available material. (Many of these libraries are open for
public use, although their primary purpose is to provide attorneys, judges, and other public officials with facilities
and resources to research law.) The addition of computer
storage capacity is aiding the struggle to master the vast
quantities of material.

Naturally, no one can have these resources at her or his
fingertips. Instead, researchers depend on indexing services, which sort out published writings and group them by
subject for easier reference. The most important of these
tools is *Shepard's Citations*, which cites, among other
things, federal and state laws; local ordinances; federal,
court, and administrative-agency decisions; and law-review
articles. For an attorney studying a particular topic, *Shepard's* will list the relevant material. Lawyers must be current with regard to the law, and only such research sources
as *Shepard's* and its brethren enable lawyers to keep up to
date.

Legal scholars have their own way of designating references. Typically, the volume number of a journal (e.g. a
law review) will come before the name of the journal. The
name will be followed by the page reference, either the
first page of the article or a particular citation. Thus, Lon
Fuller's article "The Case of the Speluncean Explorers,"
which appeared in 1949 in the sixty-second volume of the
Harvard Law Review, starting on page 616, is cited as 62
Harv. L. Rev. 616 (1949).

The same method is used for referring to court decisions. For instance, we have mentioned several times the
case of *Gideon* v. *Wainwright*, in which the Supreme
Court ruled that a defendant charged with a major crime
should have a court-appointed lawyer if he can't afford
one himself. This case is officially cited as 372 *U.S.* 335
(1963). Written out, it means that the first page of the
decision appears on page 335 of Volume 372 of the
United States Reports, a volume that reported on cases

decided in 1963. The *United States Reports* contain the opinions of the Supreme Court, published by the federal government. Other courts use other abbreviations; thus, the *Ohio Appellate Reports* are abbreviated *Ohio App.* Sometimes the volume of publications is so great that the series is renumbered by starting out all over again. For instance, in 1954 Illinois launched a new series of *Appellate Court Reports*, cited as *Ill. App. 2d.*

Few people other than lawyers ever look at opinions outside the Supreme Court. However, even in dealing with Supreme Court opinions, problems arise. The first difficulty is the fact that, in its early years, the court identified its reports not as *U.S.*, as it does now, but by the name of the court reporter who edited the publication. Thus, the case of *Marbury* v. *Madison*, in which the Supreme Court established its power of judicial review, is cited not only as 5 *U.S.* 137 (1803), but also as 1 *Cranch* 137 (1803). Beyond that, a reader must cope with two other reporting systems for the Supreme Court: the *Supreme Court Reporter* (*S. Ct.*), and the *Lawyers' Edition, Supreme Court Reports* (*L. Ed.*—since 1956 it has been *L. Ed. 2d,* i.e. a second series). These are published by private firms, who reprint the court's opinions along with supplementary matter. There are ways to convert a citation from one of these reports into the others, but it can be confusing.

Researchers need one final item, a conversion table for abbreviations. With about three thousand publications in Anglo-American legal literature, the necessity for a guide is obvious. Most of us can guess the journal identified by the abbreviation *Marijuana Rev.* But when it comes to *I. & N. Dec.* (*Immigration and Nationality Decisions*), we must find help.

For further information on these matters, we recommend Morris L. Cohen's brief introduction *Legal Research in a Nutshell* (St. Paul, 1976).

Index